Recipes for Festive Food

from Around the World

How to Make Festival Foods from Different Global

Celebrations

BY Yannick Alcorn

Copyright Warnings

Table of Contents

Introduction

Holidays and festivals exist as excuses to celebrate, but with *"Recipes for Festive Food from Around the World,"* you can craft festive feasts any time. We've compiled recipes for tantalizing dishes from around the world, so you can immerse yourself in sumptuous flavors whenever the mood strikes.

Festivals bring people together through food, but dining on traditional recipes shouldn't be limited to special occasions. With our globally inspired meal ideas, you can infuse everyday cooking with a spirit of celebration.

Discover dishes that will transport your taste buds. From simple, hearty meals to extraordinary culinary masterpieces, we provide you with an array of options. Get creative by blending cuisines and ingredients to design your own signature festival flavors.

Don't wait for a holiday to enjoy decadent meals that nourish both body and soul. Let this cookbook open your kitchen to a world of possibilities. Celebrate life's simple pleasures through the unifying power of food. Come together with loved ones to sample exotic dishes as you bond over new experiences. Every day can feel special when approached as its own distinctive festival.

AAAAAAAAAAAAAAAAAAAAAAA

1. Peanut Butter with a Monster-Like Smile

Being creative makes everyone happy. You must not wait until it is the festive season; make your family happy today by getting creative with peanut butter.

Duration: 20 minutes

Serving Size: 8

List of Ingredients:

- 8 pieces of big green apples
- 12 cups of peanut butter
- 1/2 cup of mini marshmallows

Methods:

Slice the apples using an apple slicer and remove the cores.

Spread peanut butter evenly on one side of each apple slice.

Place three pieces of marshmallows on top of the peanut butter on half of the apple slices.

Cover the marshmallow-topped slices with the remaining apple slices to create "smiling" apple sandwiches.

Repeat the process for all the apple slices.

Serve the Peanut Butter with Monster-Like Smile sandwiches.

Cooking Notes:

For best results, use fresh and firm apples to ensure easy slicing and handling.

If you don't have an apple slicer, you can use a sharp knife to cut the apples into thin slices.

Prevent Browning: To prevent the apple slices from browning before serving, you can lightly brush them with lemon juice. Lemon juice contains citric acid, which slows down the oxidation process and keeps the apples looking fresh.

Marshmallow Alternatives: If you want to explore different fillings, try substituting the marshmallows with other spreads like Nutella, chocolate spread, or almond butter. Additionally, you can add sliced bananas or strawberries to complement the peanut butter.

Grilled Option: For a warm and gooey twist, consider grilling the assembled apple sandwiches on a stovetop griddle or panini press for a few minutes on each side until the peanut butter and marshmallows melt.

Gluten-Free Option: To make this recipe gluten-free, ensure that the marshmallows you use are gluten-free certified, and double-check the peanut butter to ensure it doesn't contain any gluten-based additives.

Nut Allergy Substitutions: If you or someone you're serving has a nut allergy, you can replace the peanut butter with sunflower seed butter, soy nut butter, or even cookie butter for a unique flavor.

Freezing: These apple sandwiches can be prepared ahead of time and frozen. Wrap each sandwich individually in plastic wrap and place them in an airtight container. When you're ready to serve, let them thaw in the refrigerator for a few hours or at room temperature for a shorter time.

Presentation Tips: To enhance the presentation of your "Monster-Like Smile" sandwiches, serve them on a colorful platter with some fresh fruit or a small bowl of melted chocolate for dipping.

Texture Variations: If you prefer a bit of crunch, you can add a sprinkle of granola or chopped nuts between the peanut butter and marshmallows before assembling the sandwiches.

Slicing Variations: Instead of the traditional round apple slices, you can cut the apples into bat-shaped or other fun Halloween-themed slices for a spooky twist.

Healthier Option: If you want to make a healthier version of these sandwiches, consider using Greek yogurt or cream cheese instead of peanut butter. You can also use mini-marshmallows or cut regular marshmallows into smaller pieces to reduce the sugar content.

Remember, cooking is all about creativity and personal preference, so feel free to customize this recipe to suit your taste and the occasion. Enjoy your delicious and adorable Peanut Butter with Monster-Like Smile sandwiches!

2. Korean Style Baked Popcorn and Chicken

Every part of the world has its special festive meals, and since you can't travel all over the world to taste their meal, try this Korean recipe from your home, and you will love it.

Duration: 90 minutes

Serving Size: 8

List of Ingredients:

- 2 lb. of chicken breast, skin and bone removed and cut into cube size
- 1 cup of buttermilk
- 3 cups of cornflakes, well crushed
- 3 tbsp of soy sauce
- 3 tbsp of honey
- 1 small peeled and grated fresh ginger
- 2 tbsp of sesame oil, toasted
- 2 tbsp of sesame seeds
- 1 small green onion, well sliced
- 3 tbsp of wheat flour
- 2 tbsp of oil
- 1/3 cup of ketchup
- 1/2 cup of gochujang
- 2 tbsp of rice vinegar
- 2 cloves of well-minced garlic
- 1/2 cup of water

AAAAAAAAAAAAAAAAAAAAAA

Methods:

In a bowl, place the chicken and pour buttermilk over it. Mix thoroughly to ensure the chicken is coated with buttermilk. Cover the bowl and refrigerate for 1 hour to allow the chicken to marinate.

Preheat your oven to 400° F (about 200°C). Take two baking sheets and line them with parchment paper, setting them aside for later use.

In another bowl, combine cornflakes, flour, and pepper, mixing them well to form the coating mixture.

Remove the chicken from the buttermilk one piece at a time and dredge each piece in the corn flakes mixture until they are evenly coated.

Place the coated chicken pieces on the prepared baking sheets. Sprinkle some oil over the chicken to help with browning and moisture.

Bake the chicken in the preheated oven for approximately 20 minutes or until it is cooked thoroughly and reaches a safe internal temperature.

While the chicken is baking, prepare the Korean-style sauce in a small pan. Mix together ketchup, soy sauce, honey, ginger, rice vinegar, gochujang (Korean red chili paste), sesame oil, and water. Allow the mixture to come to a boil and simmer until the sauce thickens. Remove from heat.

Once the chicken is done baking, remove it from the oven. Brush the chicken pieces with the prepared Korean-style sauce, ensuring they are evenly coated.

Garnish the chicken with chopped green onions and sesame seeds to add flavor and visual appeal.

Serve the Korean Style Baked Popcorn and Chicken while it is still hot, and enjoy the delicious blend of flavors.

Cooking Notes:

The marinating process in buttermilk helps tenderize the chicken and adds flavor. If you don't have buttermilk, you can create a substitute by adding 1 tablespoon of lemon juice or vinegar to 1 cup of regular milk and letting it sit for 5 minutes.

To ensure even cooking, arrange the coated chicken pieces on the baking sheets without overcrowding them. Leaving some space between the pieces allows the hot air to circulate and results in crispier chicken.

Feel free to adjust the level of spiciness in the sauce by adding more or less gochujang according to your taste preferences.

Checking Chicken Doneness: To ensure that the chicken is cooked thoroughly, use a meat thermometer to check the internal temperature. The safe internal temperature for cooked chicken is 165°F (74°C).

Double Coating for Extra Crunch: For an even crunchier texture, you can try a double coating technique. After the first round of coating the chicken in the cornflake mixture, dip the coated chicken back into the buttermilk and then coat it again in the cornflake mixture before placing it on the baking sheets.

Make-Ahead Option: You can prepare the buttermilk-marinated chicken and store it in the refrigerator for up to 24 hours before baking. This allows you to marinate the chicken in advance and have a quick and delicious meal ready to bake when needed.

Freezing Instructions: If you want to freeze the chicken for future meals, you can freeze the uncooked buttermilk-marinated chicken in an airtight container. When you're ready to bake, simply thaw the chicken in the refrigerator overnight and proceed with the coating and baking steps.

Spicy Variation: If you prefer a spicier version of the Korean-style sauce, you can add a pinch of cayenne pepper or red pepper flakes to amp up the heat.

All-Purpose Dipping Sauce: The Korean-style sauce can also be served as a dipping sauce on the side. Reserve some sauce before brushing it on the chicken and serve it in a small bowl for dipping.

Smoked Paprika Flavor: Consider adding a teaspoon of smoked paprika to the cornflake mixture for a smoky and aromatic twist to the chicken's coating.

Avoiding Sticky Coating: To prevent the chicken from sticking to the baking sheets, you can lightly grease the parchment paper with cooking spray or a thin layer of oil before placing the coated chicken on them.

Crispy Skin Tip: For an extra crispy skin, you can elevate the coated chicken pieces on a wire rack placed on top of the baking sheets. This allows the hot air to circulate all around the chicken and promote even browning.

Leftover Ideas: If you have any leftovers, you can use the Korean-style chicken to make a delicious sandwich by placing it in a toasted bun with some coleslaw and pickles.

Enjoy this flavorful and crispy Korean Style Baked Popcorn and Chicken as a delightful meal option for gatherings, weeknight dinners, or even game day snacks. The combination of the crunchy coating and the savory-spicy sauce is sure to be a hit with family and friends!

3. Meatballs in a Classic Mummy Style

Have fun with kids even when it's not Halloween; make them feel special with this treat.

Duration: 30 minutes

Serving Size: 20

List of Ingredients:

- 1 can of dough sheet, refrigerated
- 1/2 cup of mustard
- 20 pieces of cooked meatballs, frozen and thawed
- 1/2 can of cooking spray

Methods:

Preheat your oven to 360° F (about 182°C).

Lightly coat a baking sheet with cooking spray and set it aside.

Unroll the dough and divide it into 4 equal parts. Then, cut each part into 10 strips.

Take a meatball and wrap two strips of dough around it, creating a bandage-like appearance. Stretch the dough gently to fully cover the meatball. Leave a small opening at the top to resemble the mummy's face.

Place the wrapped meatballs on the prepared baking sheet. Lightly spray the dough with cooking spray.

Bake the mummies in the preheated oven for about 15 minutes or until the dough turns golden brown.

Remove the mummies from the oven.

Use mustard to add two dots on each mummy's face, representing the eyes.

Serve the Meatballs in a Classic Mummy Style while they are warm and enjoy the spooky, tasty treat.

Cooking Notes:

For the meatballs, you can use your favorite meatball recipe or even store-bought meatballs to save time.

Custom Meatball Fillings: Get creative with the meatball fillings by adding different spices or herbs. For a spooky twist, you can use ground beef mixed with minced garlic, onion, and Worcestershire sauce. Alternatively, try using ground chicken, turkey, or even a plant-based meat substitute for a vegetarian version.

Cheese-Stuffed Mummies: For an extra gooey surprise, you can stuff the meatballs with small cubes of cheese, such as mozzarella or cheddar, before wrapping them with the dough. As the mummies bake, the cheese will melt, adding a delightful twist to the classic mummy style.

Puff Pastry Option: Instead of regular dough, you can use puff pastry to wrap the meatballs. Puff pastry will give the mummies a flakier texture, making them even more delicious.

Spiderweb Design: If you want to take the mummy appearance to the next level, you can use a toothpick dipped in food coloring (black or any dark color) to create a spider web pattern on the wrapped dough before baking. Draw lines radiating from the "eyes" to the edges of the dough strips and then draw circles around the "eyes" to complete the spider web effect.

Dipping Sauce: Serve the mummies with a side of marinara sauce or a tangy barbecue sauce for dipping. The sauce not only complements the meatballs but also enhances the mummy theme, resembling "bloody" or "mummy bandage" dips.

Make-Ahead Option: You can prepare the wrapped meatballs in advance and refrigerate them until you're ready to bake. This makes them an excellent party snack that can be quickly baked just before serving.

Kid-Friendly Activity: If you're cooking with kids, let them help wrap the meatballs in dough. It's a fun and engaging activity that will make the cooking process even more enjoyable.

Mummy Display: To create a spooky serving presentation, place the baked mummies on a platter with a dark-colored tablecloth. Add some plastic spiders or creepy decorations around the mummies for a complete Halloween-themed setup.

Leftover Utilization: If you have any leftover baked mummies, you can reheat them in the oven the next day to regain their crispy texture. They also make great additions to lunchboxes or as a quick snack.

These Meatballs in a Classic Mummy Style are a fun and delightful way to celebrate Halloween or any spooky-themed party. With some creativity and a few extra touches, you can transform this simple recipe into a Halloween centerpiece that everyone will enjoy!

4. Scarily Tasty Widow Cocktail

A festival can never be complete without a cocktail, and doing it by yourself sounds great. Although this is only for adults, it is tasty and will have you wanting more.

Duration: 10 minutes

Serving Size: 2

List of Ingredients:

- 5 oz of tequila
- 2 dashes of Angostura bitters
- 1 cup of blackberry-flavored water
- 1 pack of blackberries
- 1 tbsp of rosemary sprig
- 1 tbsp of lemon juice
- 2 tbsp of honey

AAAAAAAAAAAAAAAAAAAAAA

Methods:

In a cocktail mixer, combine blackberries, rosemary, honey, and lemon juice. Mix thoroughly to ensure the flavors are well combined.

Add bitters and tequila to the cocktail mixer and mix again to incorporate all the ingredients.

Filter the cocktail into a glass filled with ice to remove any solid bits and ensure a smooth texture.

Top up the drink with sparkling water to add a refreshing fizziness to the cocktail.

Garnish the cocktail with a sprig of remaining rosemary for an aromatic and visually appealing touch.

Serve the Scarily Tasty Widow Cocktail and enjoy its spooky yet delightful flavors.

Cooking Notes:

To make the cocktail even more chilling, you can prepare the blackberries and rosemary in advance and store them in the refrigerator. Chilled ingredients will enhance the overall taste and presentation of the cocktail.

Adjust the sweetness of the cocktail by adding more or less honey and lemon juice according to your taste preferences.

Blackberry Variations: While fresh blackberries are ideal for this cocktail, you can also use frozen blackberries. Thaw them before using and save any excess juice from the thawing process to add an extra burst of blackberry flavor to the drink.

Infused Ice Cubes: For an elegant presentation and enhanced flavor, consider using infused ice cubes. Add a few blackberries and small sprigs of rosemary to each compartment of an ice cube tray, then fill with water and freeze. These infused ice cubes will slowly release their flavors as they melt into the cocktail.

Rim Variation: If you want to add a spooky touch, you can coat the rim of the glass with blackberry juice or lemon juice and dip it into black sugar or crushed graham crackers for a "black widow" look.

Simple Syrup Substitute: Instead of honey, you can use simple syrup to sweeten the cocktail. To make simple syrup, mix equal parts water and granulated sugar in a saucepan and heat until the sugar dissolves. Let it cool before using in the cocktail.

Herb Substitutions: If you can't find rosemary or prefer a different herb, you can experiment with other options like thyme or basil. Each herb will lend a unique flavor profile to the cocktail.

Muddling Technique: When muddling the blackberries and rosemary, be gentle to avoid over-extracting bitter compounds from the herbs. Lightly press and twist to release the flavors without bruising the herbs.

Chilling the Cocktail: If you prefer your cocktails extra chilled, you can shake all the ingredients together with ice in the cocktail mixer or shaker before filtering into the serving glass.

Cocktail Presentation: Serve the Scarily Tasty Widow Cocktail in a stylish cocktail glass or even a mason jar for a rustic touch. Add a blackberry and rosemary skewer as a final garnish for an exquisite appearance.

Make-It-a-Pitcher Option: To serve a larger group, you can scale up the recipe and mix the cocktail in a pitcher. This way, you can easily prepare multiple servings in advance for a party or gathering.

Mocktail Option: For a family-friendly version, prepare a non-alcoholic mocktail using sparkling water, blackberries, rosemary, lemon juice, and honey. The mocktail still delivers the delightful flavors without the alcohol.

With its vibrant colors and aromatic combination of blackberries and rosemary, the Scarily Tasty Widow Cocktail is the perfect Halloween or spooky-themed drink. Adjust the sweetness and customize the presentation to your liking, and get ready to impress your guests with this hauntingly delicious concoction!

5. Bowls Loaded with Burger

Want to have fun from the comfort of your home? This is a perfect meal to gather everyone together and let them pile their favorite toppings of burgers in their bowls.

Duration: 30 minutes

Serving Size: 4

List of Ingredients:

- 1/2 tbsp of onion powder
- 1/2 tbsp of paprika
- 2 tbsp of mayo
- 1 tbsp of ketchup
- 1 tsp of yellow mustard
- 1 pint of tomatoes cut in halves
- 1/2 cup of well-sliced dill pickle
- 1/2 cup of well-sliced onions
- 1/2 cup of cheddar cheese, shredded
- 2 well-chopped cube sized hamburger buns
- 1 pound of ground turkey
- 1/2 tbsp of garlic powder
- 1/2 tsp of oregano, dried
- 1/2 tsp of salt
- 1/2 tsp of black pepper
- 1 tbsp of pickle juice
- 1 head of well-chopped romaine

AAAAAAAAAAAAAAAAAAAAAA

Methods:

Preheat your oven to 360° F (about 182°C).

Spread the hamburger cubes on a baking sheet and bake them in the preheated oven for approximately 15 minutes or until they turn golden brown. Once done, set them aside.

Heat a pan over medium heat and add ground turkey, onion powder, garlic, paprika, oregano, pepper, and salt. Cook the turkey while stirring frequently to break it into smaller pieces for the meat sauce.

While the turkey is cooking, prepare the sauce in a bowl by mixing ketchup, mayo, pickle juice, mustard, remaining onion and garlic powder, and paprika. Stir well until all the ingredients are thoroughly combined.

Divide the romaine lettuce into 4 separate bowls, creating a base for each serving.

Top each bowl of romaine lettuce with the cooked ground turkey, tomatoes, and pickles.

Pour the prepared sauce over the meat and toppings to add a flavorful and tangy kick to the dish.

Serve the Bowls Loaded with Burger and enjoy the delicious combination of flavors.

Cooking Notes:

You can use pre-made hamburger cubes or cut pieces of cooked burger patties for this recipe.

For ground meat, you have the flexibility to choose between turkey, chicken, beef, or plant-based alternatives like tofu or lentils, depending on your dietary preferences.

Crispy Burger Cubes: To achieve a crispy texture for the hamburger cubes, toss them with a little oil and seasonings (such as salt and pepper) before baking. This will help them develop a golden and crunchy crust.

Bun Croutons: If you want to mimic the taste and texture of burger buns in the salad, you can cut hamburger buns or bread into small cubes, toss them with a little oil and seasonings, and then toast them in the oven until they become croutons. Add these bun croutons to the salad for a fun twist.

Grilled Meat Option: Instead of baking the hamburger cubes, you can grill them for a smokier flavor. Preheat your grill to medium-high heat and cook the hamburger cubes on skewers or a grill pan until they are charred and cooked through.

Tomato Varieties: Experiment with different tomato varieties to add color and flavor to the dish. You can use cherry tomatoes, grape tomatoes, or heirloom tomatoes, depending on what's available and your personal preference.

Pickle Choices: Get creative with pickles by using different types like dill pickles, bread and butter pickles, or spicy pickles. Each type will bring a unique tanginess to the Bowls Loaded with Burger.

Lettuce Options: While romaine lettuce provides a sturdy base for the dish, you can use other greens like spinach, kale, or mixed salad greens for added nutritional value and texture variation.

Crunchy Toppings: For extra crunch, consider adding toppings like crushed tortilla chips, crumbled bacon, or toasted nuts to the salad.

Make-Ahead: You can prepare the meat sauce and sauce in advance and store them in separate containers in the refrigerator. Assemble the salad just before serving for a quick and convenient meal.

Gluten-Free Option: To make this dish gluten-free, ensure that the sauces and condiments you use, such as ketchup, mayo, and mustard, are gluten-free certified.

Vegan/Vegetarian Variation: For a plant-based version, use ground plant-based meat substitutes like Beyond Meat or Impossible Burger. Also, substitute vegan mayo for regular mayo in the sauce, and use dairy-free cheese if desired.

The Bowls Loaded with Burger can be a versatile and satisfying meal option with various customizable elements. Tailor the ingredients and seasonings to your liking and enjoy a delicious salad that captures the flavors of a classic burger in a healthier and more nutritious way.

6. Bagel in Quiche Form

It's time to have a festival in your home; make this tasty bagel and have fun with your family.

Duration: 2 hours 20 minutes

Serving Size: 6

List of Ingredients:

- 1 tbsp of festival bagel seasoning
- 1 tbsp of sour cream
- 1/2 tsp of salt
- 3 medium-sized green onions, well sliced
- 1 small thinly sliced red onion
- 1 tbsp of capers, drained
- 1 tbsp of fresh dill, well chopped
- 1 lb. smoked salmon, well sliced
- 1 pie crust
- 6 large eggs
- 1/3 cup of half and half
- 1/2 tsp of black pepper
- 1 tsp of lemon juice

AAAAAAAAAAAAAAAAAAAAAA

Methods:

Unroll the pie crust and sprinkle age seasoning on one side. Roll the seasoning into the crust using a rolling pin.

Place the seasoned pie crust into a pie dish with the seasoned side facing up. Let it chill in the refrigerator for about 30 minutes to prevent shrinking during baking.

Preheat your oven to 360° F (about 182°C). Place the pie dough on a baking sheet lined with parchment paper and bake for 15 minutes. Then, remove from the oven, prick any air bubbles, and bake again for an additional 19 minutes. Remove from the oven and set aside.

In a bowl, whisk together eggs, sour cream, half and half, salt, and pepper until well combined. Add green onions and whisk again to incorporate them into the mixture.

Pour the egg mixture onto the pre-baked crust in the pie dish.

Bake the quiche in the preheated oven for about 90 minutes or until it is set in the middle. Once done, remove it from the oven and place it on a wire rack to cool.

In a small bowl, mix lemon juice, red onions, dill, and capers together to create a flavorful topping for the quiche.

Once the quiche has cooled slightly, top it with the lemony onion and caper mixture, and serve it alongside smoked salmon for a delicious Bagel in Quiche Form experience.

Cooking Notes:

Age seasoning typically contains ingredients like black and white sesame seeds, poppy seeds, dried garlic, and dried onion. If you don't have age seasoning, you can use a combination of these individual spices to create a similar flavor profile.

Chilling the pie crust before baking helps relax the gluten and prevents it from shrinking while baking.

Custom Quiche Fillings: While this recipe includes green onions, feel free to customize the quiche with additional ingredients like sautéed vegetables, cooked bacon or sausage, diced ham, spinach, mushrooms, or grated cheese. Be mindful of the quantity of fillings to ensure they don't overpower the delicate flavor of the smoked salmon topping.

Preparing the Salmon: To enhance the presentation of the smoked salmon topping, you can roll or fold the slices into rosettes or create decorative shapes. This adds an elegant touch to the quiche.

Crust Variations: If you prefer a gluten-free option or want to try a different crust, you can use a gluten-free pie crust or experiment with other types of crusts, such as a buttery shortcrust or a flaky puff pastry.

Substitution for Half and Half: If you don't have half and half, you can create a substitute by combining equal parts whole milk and heavy cream. This will still provide a creamy texture and richness to the quiche.

Make-Ahead Option: This quiche can be prepared ahead of time and reheated when needed. After baking and cooling, wrap the quiche tightly in plastic wrap and store it in the refrigerator for up to 2-3 days. Reheat individual slices in the oven or microwave before serving.

Freezing Instructions: You can freeze the quiche for longer storage. Wrap the cooled quiche securely in plastic wrap and aluminum foil to prevent freezer burn. Thaw the quiche in the refrigerator overnight before reheating.

Herb Variations: Feel free to experiment with different herbs in the lemony onion and caper mixture. Dill complements the smoked salmon well, but you can also try parsley, chives, or tarragon for alternative flavor combinations.

Adding Cream Cheese: For a richer and creamier quiche, consider adding small dollops of cream cheese on top of the egg mixture before baking. The cream cheese will melt and blend into the quiche, adding an extra layer of indulgence.

Quiche Serving Size: Depending on your preference, you can make individual mini-quiches using smaller pie dishes or ramekins. This allows for easy portion control and makes for an elegant presentation when serving guests.

Pairing Recommendations: To complete the Bagel in Quiche Form experience, serve the quiche with classic bagel toppings like capers, cream cheese, red onion slices, and fresh dill. This will enhance the bagel-inspired theme and create a delightful brunch spread.

The Bagel in Quiche Form offers a unique and delicious twist on the traditional quiche, making it a delightful addition to any brunch or special occasion. Tailor the fillings and toppings to your liking, and enjoy this savory and flavorful dish with family and friends!

7. Puffs and Cabbage in Cream

These little cream puffs which are called choux in French, are an amazing way to start a festive period. They taste even better when you bake them.

Duration: 60 minutes

Serving Size: 12

List of Ingredients:

- 2 cups of flour already sifted
- 5 big eggs
- 1/2 cup of pastry cream
- 2 cups of water
- 1 tbsp of sugar
- 1/2 tsp of salt
- 1/2 cup of butter

AAAAAAAAAAAAAAAAAAAAAAA

Methods:

Pour water into a pot and add salt, sugar, and butter. Bring it to a boil until the butter dissolves completely.

Stir in the flour to form dough and continue cooking for 1 minute, while stirring continuously.

Remove the pot from the heat and transfer the dough into a mixer. Let it cool slightly before mixing in 4 eggs until the mixture becomes smooth.

Grease a baking sheet and spoon the dough onto it. Place the sheet in the oven and bake for approximately 30 minutes.

In the meantime, crack one of the remaining eggs and separate the egg white. Use the egg white to glaze the puffs before returning them to the oven to achieve a golden-brown color.

Once the puffs are ready, take them out of the oven and let them cool down.

Slice the cooled puffs in half and fill them with your desired pastry cream before serving.

Cooking Notes:

Be careful when adding the flour to the boiling water-butter mixture, and ensure you stir constantly to prevent lumps from forming.

Piping the Dough: For more consistent and evenly sized puffs, consider using a piping bag fitted with a large round tip to shape the dough on the baking sheet. This will also give the puffs a neater appearance.

Egg Glaze Variations: Instead of using only egg whites for glazing, you can mix the egg white with a splash of milk or water to create a more delicate and evenly spreadable glaze. Alternatively, you can use a whole beaten egg for a richer color and shine.

Flavoring the Dough: Add a hint of flavor to the dough by incorporating a teaspoon of vanilla extract, almond extract, or citrus zest (lemon or orange). These additions will complement various pastry cream fillings and enhance the overall taste.

Proper Cooling: Allow the baked puffs to cool completely on a wire rack before slicing and filling. This prevents them from becoming soggy due to trapped steam.

Filling Options: Experiment with different pastry cream flavors, such as vanilla, chocolate, coffee, or fruit-flavored creams, to offer a variety of options. You can also try sweet whipped cream, custards, fruit preserves, or Nutella as fillings.

Hollowing the Puffs: To create more space for filling, use a small paring knife to carefully hollow out the center of each puff. This will allow you to add a generous amount of filling without overwhelming the dough.

Freezing the Puffs: These cream puffs freeze well and can be prepared in advance for later enjoyment. After baking and cooling, store the unfilled puffs in an airtight container in the freezer. Thaw them at room temperature before filling and serving.

Serving Presentation: To serve the cream puffs in an elegant and appealing manner, dust them with powdered sugar or drizzle them with melted chocolate before serving. This adds a touch of finesse and makes them even more irresistible.

Flavor Pairings: When choosing fillings, think about complementing flavors. For instance, pair fruit fillings with vanilla pastry cream or chocolate fillings with coffee-flavored pastry cream for a harmonious taste experience.

Savory Puff Variations: If you prefer savory puffs, you can omit the sugar from the dough and use a savory filling, such as chicken and mushroom, spinach and feta, or ham and cheese. These savory cream puffs are perfect for appetizers or a light lunch option.

With these cooking notes, you can confidently make delectable cream puffs with various fillings to suit your taste and occasion. Whether you're creating sweet treats or savory delights, these versatile puffs are sure to impress and satisfy any palate.

8. Creamy Pumpkin Muffins with Pecan

Step away from usual meals, and serve this as a perfect breakfast from the comfort of your home. This is the perfect fall holiday meal.

Duration: 90 minutes

Serving Size: 10

List of Ingredients:

- 2 cups of flour
- 1 tsp of cinnamon, ground
- 1/3 tbsp of baking soda
- 1/3 tbsp of salt
- 1/2 tsp of nutmeg, ground
- 1/2 tsp of cloves, ground
- 2 medium-sized eggs
- 1 can of pumpkin puree
- 1 can of crunchy pecan
- 1/2 cup of softened cream cheese
- 2 tbsp of sugar
- 1 tbsp of oil
- 1/2 tsp of baking powder
- 1/2 cup of brown sugar
- 1/2 cup of oil, canola

AAAAAAAAAAAAAAAAAAAAAA

Methods:

In a bowl, mix sugar and cream cheese together. Cover the mixture and freeze it for 30 minutes.

Preheat your oven to 350° F (175° C). Grease a 10-cup muffin tin with oil and line each cup with muffin liners.

In a separate bowl, combine flour, baking soda, baking powder, cinnamon, salt, nutmeg, and cloves.

In another bowl, use a hand mixer to thoroughly blend eggs, canola oil, brown sugar, and pumpkin puree. Gradually add the flour mixture to the wet ingredients and mix until well combined.

Spoon the muffin batter into each muffin cup, filling each about halfway. Add a dollop of the cream cheese mixture on top of the batter in each cup. Add another layer of batter to cover the cream cheese.

Sprinkle pecans on top of each muffin for added flavor and crunch.

Bake the muffins in the preheated oven for approximately 30 minutes or until a toothpick inserted into the center comes out clean.

Allow the muffins to cool slightly in the muffin tin before removing them and letting them cool completely on a wire rack.

Serve the creamy pumpkin muffins with pecans at room temperature or slightly warm.

Cooking Notes:

Make sure the cream cheese is soft and at room temperature before mixing it with sugar. This will ensure a smoother and easier blending process.

When lining the muffin tin with liners, you can also lightly grease the liners to prevent the muffins from sticking.

Pumpkin Puree Substitution: If you don't have canned pumpkin puree, you can use homemade pumpkin puree. To make your own, roast or boil fresh pumpkin until tender, then puree it in a blender or food processor until smooth.

Cream Cheese Variations: For a twist on the cream cheese filling, consider adding a dash of vanilla extract or a sprinkle of pumpkin pie spice to the mixture. This will enhance the cream cheese flavor and complement the pumpkin spice in the muffins.

Streusel Topping: For added texture and sweetness, create a streusel topping by mixing together flour, butter, brown sugar, and a pinch of cinnamon. Sprinkle the streusel on top of the muffins before baking for a delicious crumbly crust.

Chopped Apples: To add extra moistness and a burst of flavor, consider incorporating small chunks of diced apples into the muffin batter. This complements the pumpkin and spices wonderfully.

Filling Variations: Instead of using cream cheese, you can fill the muffins with a caramel sauce or a pumpkin spice cream filling for a more decadent treat.

Make-Ahead and Storage: These muffins are great for meal prep. Once cooled completely, store them in an airtight container at room temperature for up to 3 days or in the refrigerator for up to 5 days. They can also be frozen for up to 2 months.

Serving Accompaniments: Serve these creamy pumpkin muffins with pecans alongside a warm cup of coffee, tea, or hot chocolate for a delightful autumn treat.

Mini Muffin Option: If you prefer bite-sized treats, you can use a mini muffin tin and adjust the baking time accordingly (about 12-15 minutes).

Nut-Free Option: If you or your guests have nut allergies, you can omit the pecans or replace them with pumpkin seeds or sunflower seeds for added crunch.

Custom Toppings: For a more festive presentation, top each muffin with a small dollop of whipped cream and a sprinkle of cinnamon or a drizzle of caramel sauce.

These creamy pumpkin muffins with pecans are a delectable autumn delight, perfect for breakfast, brunch, or a sweet treat any time of the day. With the additional cooking notes, you have the flexibility to customize the flavors and presentation to suit your taste and preference. Enjoy the warm, cozy flavors of pumpkin and spices in every bite!

9. Cheese and Baked Chicken

Step away from your usual fatty fried chicken and try baking your chicken. This meal is mostly served during special occasions; however, you don't need to wait for a celebration period, and you can make any moment special with your family and the meal.

Duration: 30 minutes

Serving Size: 8

List of Ingredients:

- 2 cloves of garlic, well minced
- 1 tsp of ground cumin
- 1 can of drained green chilies
- 1/2 cup of pepper jack cheese, shredded
- 4 cups of lettuce, shredded
- 1 cup of plain yogurt
- 1 diced avocado
- 1/2 cup of cilantro
- 1/2 can of cooking spray
- 4 pounds of shredded chicken
- 1/2 cup of salsa
- 8 pieces of whole wheat flour tortilla
- 1/3 cup of Pico de Gallo

AAAAAAAAAAAAAAAAAAAAAA

Methods:

Preheat your oven to 360° F (182° C) and spray a baking sheet with cooking spray. Set it aside.

In a bowl, mix the chicken, garlic, salsa, cumin, and chilies together to create a flavorful filling.

Take a tortilla and place a portion of the chicken mixture onto the bottom of it. Sprinkle some cheese on top of the filling. Carefully lift the edge of the tortilla closest to you and wrap it around the filling. Fold in the sides and continue rolling until you have a little cylinder-shaped wrap. Repeat this process for all the tortillas.

Place the filled tortillas on the prepared baking sheet and bake in the preheated oven for approximately 20 minutes or until they become crispy and golden brown.

While the tortillas are baking, prepare your toppings. On a plate, arrange some lettuce as the base. Once the tortillas are done, place them on top of the lettuce.

Finally, add Pico de Gallo, yogurt, avocado slices, and cilantro on top of the baked tortillas.

Serve the Cheese and Baked Chicken wraps immediately, and enjoy!

Cooking Notes:

Make sure to evenly distribute the chicken mixture and cheese across the tortillas for consistent flavor in each wrap.

Shredded Chicken Option: For a quicker preparation, you can use pre-cooked and shredded chicken. Rotisserie chicken works well and saves time. Simply mix the shredded chicken with the salsa, garlic, cumin, and chilies to create the filling.

Tortilla Size: The size of tortillas can vary, so adjust the filling amount accordingly to avoid overstuffing or underfilling the wraps. Aim for a balanced ratio of filling to tortilla for the best taste experience.

Tortilla Variations: Experiment with different types of tortillas to suit your preferences or dietary needs. You can use whole wheat tortillas, corn tortillas, spinach or tomato-flavored tortillas, or gluten-free tortillas as alternatives.

Tortilla Warmers: To keep the tortillas warm and pliable while assembling the wraps, use a tortilla warmer or wrap them in a clean kitchen towel. This helps prevent them from becoming stiff and cracking during assembly.

Cheese Selection: You can use a blend of cheeses like cheddar, Monterey Jack, or a Mexican cheese blend for added flavor. Grated pepper jack cheese can add a bit of spiciness if desired.

Sauce Options: Instead of yogurt, you can use sour cream, guacamole, or a drizzle of hot sauce to add a creamy or tangy element to the wraps.

Grilled or Pan-Fried Option: For a different twist on the recipe, consider grilling or pan-frying the assembled wraps instead of baking. This will give the tortillas a crispier texture and a slight char.

Leftovers: If you have leftover chicken filling or toppings, save them to use in salads, quesadillas, or as a filling for another batch of wraps.

Make-Ahead Option: You can prepare the chicken filling and toppings in advance and store them separately in the refrigerator. Assemble and bake the wraps just before serving for a quick and easy meal.

Serving Suggestion: These Cheese and Baked Chicken wraps pair well with a side of Mexican rice or a fresh fruit salad for a complete and satisfying meal.

With these cooking notes, you can confidently create delicious and customizable Cheese and Baked Chicken wraps with a refreshing Pico de Gallo topping. Whether you're making a quick weeknight dinner or serving a crowd, these wraps are sure to be a hit!

10. Grilled Spicy Lobster Tail

Enjoy your lobster this festive period and get your guests wanting more.

Duration: 30 minutes

Serving Size: 5

List of Ingredients:

- 5 pieces of lobster tails
- 1/2 tsp of salt
- 1/2 cup of melted butter
- 1/2 cup of lemon wedges
- 1 tbsp of oil
- 1/2 tsp of ground black pepper

AAAAAAAAAAAAAAAAAAAAAA

Methods:

Preheat your grill to the desired temperature.

Brush the lobster tails with oil and season them with salt and pepper according to your taste preferences.

Place the seasoned lobster tails on the preheated grill and cook them for approximately 5 minutes on one side. Then, flip them over and brush with melted butter. Continue grilling for another 5 minutes or until the lobster is thoroughly cooked.

Once the lobster tails are done, remove them from the grill.

Serve the Grilled Spicy Lobster Tails with additional melted butter and lemon wedges on the side for added flavor.

Cooking Notes:

To enhance the spiciness, you can add a pinch of cayenne pepper or red pepper flakes to the oil before brushing it onto the lobster tails.

Make sure the grill is adequately preheated to achieve proper searing and cooking of the lobster tails.

Grilling time may vary depending on the size and thickness of the lobster tails. Adjust the cooking time accordingly to avoid overcooking, as lobster meat can become tough and chewy if cooked for too long.

Grilling Lobster Shell-Side Down: To prevent the lobster tails from curling up and to ensure even cooking, start grilling them with the shell-side down. This helps keep the meat flat on the grill surface.

Basting with Butter: While grilling, baste the lobster tails with melted butter every few minutes to keep them moist and to add a rich, buttery flavor. The butter also helps to enhance the charred and smoky taste from the grill.

Grilling with Citrus: For an additional burst of flavor, you can place lemon or lime slices directly on the grill alongside the lobster tails. Grilling the citrus adds a slightly smoky and tangy essence to complement the lobster.

Doneness Test: To check if the lobster tails are fully cooked, insert an instant-read thermometer into the thickest part of the tail meat. The internal temperature should reach 140°F (60°C) for perfectly cooked lobster.

Herb Infusion: Before grilling, consider infusing the oil used for brushing with herbs like thyme, rosemary, or tarragon. This will infuse the lobster tails with subtle herb flavors while they cook.

Custom Spice Blend: Create your own spice blend by combining salt, pepper, garlic powder, onion powder, and any other spices you enjoy. This allows you to tailor the flavor profile to your liking.

Soaking Wooden Skewers: If you prefer grilling lobster tails on skewers for ease of handling, use wooden skewers and soak them in water for about 30 minutes before grilling. This prevents them from burning while on the grill.

Grilling Presentation: For an attractive presentation, serve the grilled lobster tails on a platter with fresh herbs, such as parsley or cilantro, and additional lemon wedges for garnish.

Pairing Recommendations: Grilled lobster tails pair wonderfully with a variety of side dishes, such as grilled vegetables, garlic butter roasted potatoes, or a refreshing green salad with citrus vinaigrette.

Butter Dipping Sauce: Offer a variety of flavored butter dipping sauces on the side. Consider garlic butter, lemon-basil butter, or a chili-lime butter to provide guests with options for customizing their lobster experience.

With these additional cooking notes, you can confidently grill delicious and succulent Spicy Lobster Tails that are sure to impress your guests or make for an elegant seafood dinner at home. Enjoy the delightful smoky and spicy flavors of this dish, perfect for a special occasion or a memorable meal.

11. Baked Cinnamon Roll

This is one simple meal that everyone is bound to enjoy during this festive period. You can decide to make it a breakfast date dish with your family.

Duration: 40 minutes

Serving Size: 10

List of Ingredients:

- 4 large eggs
- 1 cup of skimmed milk
- 1 tsp of vanilla extract
- 1 tbsp of oil
- 3 cans of cinnamon rolls with icing, chopped
- 1 tbsp of maple syrup

AAAAAAAAAAAAAAAAAAAAAA

Methods:

Preheat your oven to 380° F (193° C) and grease a baking sheet with oil.

Arrange the cinnamon rolls on the greased baking sheet.

In a bowl, mix together the eggs, vanilla, and milk. Pour the mixture over the cinnamon rolls, ensuring they are well coated.

Place the baking sheet with the coated cinnamon rolls in the preheated oven. Bake for approximately 25 minutes or until the cinnamon rolls turn golden brown.

Once the cinnamon rolls are done baking, remove them from the oven.

Allow the baked cinnamon rolls to cool for about 10 minutes.

After cooling, sprinkle the cinnamon rolls with maple syrup for added sweetness.

Serve the delicious Baked Cinnamon Rolls while they are still warm and enjoy!

Cooking Notes:

When greasing the baking sheet, you can use butter or cooking spray to prevent the cinnamon rolls from sticking.

Make sure the oven is properly preheated to ensure even baking and a golden-brown crust on the cinnamon rolls.

While mixing the eggs, vanilla, and milk, whisk the ingredients together thoroughly to ensure a consistent coating for the cinnamon rolls.

Customizing the Toppings: Apart from maple syrup or glaze, you can experiment with various toppings to enhance the flavor and presentation of the baked cinnamon rolls. Consider adding a sprinkle of chopped nuts, such as pecans or walnuts, for a delightful crunch. You can also use a dusting of powdered sugar or a dollop of whipped cream for an extra touch of sweetness.

Adding Fruits: To incorporate a fruity twist to the baked cinnamon rolls, add sliced bananas, diced apples, or berries on top before baking. The fruits will caramelize and infuse the rolls with natural sweetness.

Cream Cheese Frosting: Instead of a simple glaze, consider using a cream cheese frosting to make the cinnamon rolls even more indulgent. Mix softened cream cheese, powdered sugar, vanilla extract, and a splash of milk until smooth, and drizzle it over the warm rolls.

Caramel Drizzle: For a decadent treat, drizzle warm caramel sauce over the baked cinnamon rolls. The combination of cinnamon and caramel creates a delightful flavor contrast.

Make-Ahead Preparation: You can prepare the egg-milk mixture and store it in the refrigerator overnight. In the morning, simply pour the chilled mixture over the cinnamon rolls and bake as usual. This makes for a convenient and quick breakfast option.

Testing Doneness: To ensure the cinnamon rolls are fully baked, insert a toothpick into the center of one roll. It should come out clean or with a few moist crumbs clinging to it.

Icing Variation: If you prefer a creamier icing, mix powdered sugar, milk, and a splash of vanilla extract to make a simple vanilla icing. Drizzle it over the baked cinnamon rolls while they are still warm.

Leftover Storage: If you have any leftover baked cinnamon rolls, store them in an airtight container at room temperature for up to 2 days. Reheat them in the microwave or oven to enjoy the next day.

Frozen Cinnamon Rolls: If using store-bought frozen cinnamon rolls, follow the package instructions for baking. Once baked, you can still use the egg-milk mixture and add toppings to customize the flavor.

Serving Suggestion: For a complete and satisfying breakfast or brunch, serve the baked cinnamon rolls alongside a cup of freshly brewed coffee, hot chocolate, or a glass of cold milk.

With these additional cooking notes, you can create delectable and customizable Baked Cinnamon Rolls with your favorite toppings and glazes. Whether you enjoy them for breakfast, brunch, or as a sweet treat any time of the day, these warm and comforting rolls are sure to be a hit!

12. Baked Casserole and Green Bean

This is one dish everyone wants to eat during a festival, and most people travel to another city just to have this meal. However, using our recipe, you can prepare an amazing dish even when it's not a festive period.

Duration: 40 minutes

Serving Size: 5

List of Ingredients:

- 1/2 tsp of black pepper
- 2 cans of drained green beans
- 1 cup of fried onions
- 1 can of mushroom soup of condensed cream
- 1/2 cup of milk
- 1/2 tbsp of soy sauce

AAAAAAAAAAAAAAAAAAAAAA

Methods:

Preheat your oven to 360° F (182° C).

In a casserole dish, combine mushroom soup, soy sauce, pepper, and part of the chopped onions with green beans.

Place the casserole in the preheated oven and bake for approximately 30 minutes, or until the mixture starts to bubble. Stir the mixture to ensure even cooking and distribution of flavors. Add the remaining chopped onions.

Continue baking for another 5 minutes to allow the flavors to meld together.

Once done, remove the Baked Casserole and Green Bean from the oven.

Serve the delicious casserole warm and enjoy!

Cooking Notes:

For a creamier texture, you can use condensed mushroom soup instead of regular mushroom soup.

If you prefer a richer flavor, you can sauté the chopped onions before adding them to the casserole. This will bring out their sweetness and add depth to the dish.

Optionally, you can add other vegetables or ingredients to the casserole, such as sliced mushrooms, garlic, or bacon, to enhance the taste and texture.

Adjust the seasoning according to your taste. You can add more soy sauce, salt, or pepper to suit your preferences.

Blanching Green Beans: To ensure the green beans are tender and vibrant in color, you can blanch them in boiling water for 1-2 minutes before adding them to the casserole. This helps retain their texture and color during baking.

Homemade Mushroom Soup: For a homemade touch, you can make your own mushroom soup using fresh mushrooms, onions, garlic, broth, and cream. Simply sauté the mushrooms and onions, add flour to create a roux, then gradually add broth and cream until the soup thickens. Use this homemade soup as a base for the casserole.

Cheese Options: If you enjoy cheesy casseroles, consider adding shredded cheddar, mozzarella, or Swiss cheese to the casserole. The cheese will melt into the dish, adding a delightful gooey and savory element.

Herb Infusion: For added aroma and flavor, include dried herbs like thyme, rosemary, or parsley. Sprinkle them over the casserole before baking or mix them into the mushroom soup mixture.

Breadcrumb Topping Variation: Instead of cheese, you can create a breadcrumb topping by mixing breadcrumbs with melted butter and your favorite herbs. Sprinkle the breadcrumb mixture over the casserole for a crunchy and savory crust.

Using Fresh Green Beans: If fresh green beans are in season, you can use them instead of canned or frozen ones. Trim the ends and blanch them briefly before adding them to the casserole.

Preparing in Advance: You can assemble the casserole ahead of time and refrigerate it until you're ready to bake it. When ready, simply bake it as instructed, adding a few extra minutes to the baking time if needed.

Serving with Protein: To make this casserole a complete meal, serve it alongside grilled chicken, turkey, or your favorite protein source. This adds variety and makes the dish more satisfying.

Caramelized Onion Topping: For an extra touch of sweetness and depth of flavor, caramelize some onions separately and use them as a topping for the casserole.

Vegetarian-Friendly: This casserole is already vegetarian-friendly, but you can also make it vegan by using plant-based cream of mushroom soup and tamari instead of soy sauce.

With these additional cooking notes, you have the freedom to customize and elevate the Baked Casserole and Green Bean dish to suit your taste preferences and dietary needs. Enjoy this classic and comforting casserole as a delightful side dish or a hearty main course for your next family gathering or holiday feast!

13. Rice and Chicken Soup in the Peruvian Style

Another wonderful soup for a cold winter holiday with lots of fresh veggies to go with. You don't actually need to travel all the way down to Peruvian or South America; you can prepare this meal from the comfort of your home using our recipe.

Duration: 30 minutes

Serving Size: 6

List of Ingredients:

- 1 bell of Serrano pepper well minced and seeded
- 5 cloves of well-minced garlic
- 5 cups of chicken broth
- 3 pieces of well-diced potatoes
- 1 cup of brown rice
- 1 can of cilantro
- 1 tbsp of lime juice
- 1 tbsp of cumin
- 1/2 tsp of salt
- 1/2 tsp of black pepper
- 2 tbsp of oil
- 1 piece of diced poblano pepper
- 1 medium-sized well diced yellow pepper
- 2 big peeled and diced carrots
- 2 cups of cooked shredded chicken
- 1 cup of water
- 1/2 cup of frozen peas

AAAAAAAAAAAAAAAAAAAAAA

Methods:

In a large pan, heat oil over medium heat. Add poblano and onions, then simmer for 5 minutes until softened. Next, add Serrano peppers and garlic, and simmer for another 2 minutes. Remove from heat and set aside.

In a separate pot, pour chicken broth and add potatoes, carrots, rice, and chicken. Bring it to a boil and let it simmer until the rice is fully cooked.

While the rice and veggies are cooking, transfer the pepper mixture (from step 1) into a blender. Let it cool a bit before adding lime juice, cilantro, and water to the blender. Blend the mixture until it becomes smooth.

Once the rice and veggies are cooked, add the blended cilantro mixture, along with peas, into the pot. Cook until the peas are heated through.

Remove the pot from the heat, season the soup with pepper and salt according to taste.

Serve the delicious Peruvian-style Rice and Chicken Soup hot and enjoy!

Cooking Notes:

Poblano peppers and Serrano peppers can vary in heat level, so adjust the amount according to your preference for spiciness.

When blending the pepper mixture, ensure it has cooled down a bit to avoid any accidents due to hot liquid splattering.

Feel free to customize the soup with additional vegetables like corn or bell peppers for added flavor and nutrition.

Chicken Broth Alternatives: If you prefer a vegetarian version of the Peruvian-style Rice and Chicken Soup, you can use vegetable broth instead of chicken broth. This will result in a flavorful and satisfying vegetarian soup option.

Preparing the Chicken: You can use pre-cooked shredded chicken for convenience or cook boneless, skinless chicken breasts in the broth for added tenderness. Simply shred the cooked chicken before adding it to the soup.

Rice Options: While the recipe calls for rice, you can experiment with different varieties such as long-grain white rice, brown rice, or even quinoa for a nutritious twist. Adjust the cooking time accordingly based on the type of rice or grain you choose.

Consistency Adjustment: If you find the soup too thick, you can add more chicken broth or water to achieve your desired consistency. Conversely, if you prefer a thicker soup, let it simmer for a bit longer to reduce and thicken the broth.

Additional Seasonings: Consider adding spices like cumin or smoked paprika to the pepper mixture for added depth of flavor. You can also add a bay leaf while simmering the broth for an earthy aroma.

Garnish Ideas: Besides cilantro and lime juice, you can garnish the soup with avocado slices, chopped green onions, or a dollop of sour cream for added creaminess and tanginess.

Using Frozen Peas: If using frozen peas, add them to the soup in the final minutes of cooking to prevent them from becoming too soft. This ensures the peas maintain their texture and vibrant green color.

Preparing in Advance: This soup tastes even better the next day as the flavors meld together. Consider making a larger batch and store the leftovers in the refrigerator for a quick and delicious meal later.

Serving Accompaniments: Serve the Peruvian-style Rice and Chicken Soup with crusty bread or warm tortillas on the side for a complete and satisfying meal.

Kid-Friendly Adaptation: To make the soup more kid-friendly, you can reduce the spiciness by using fewer Serrano peppers or omitting them altogether. Kids will still enjoy the vibrant flavors of the soup without the heat.

With these additional cooking notes, you can confidently prepare a flavorful and comforting Peruvian-style Rice and Chicken Soup that suits your taste preferences and dietary needs. This soup is a wonderful combination of textures and tastes, perfect for warming up on chilly days or enjoying any time you crave a comforting bowl of soup.

14. Meatball Sandwich

This is a special meal from Vietnam, and it is mostly served as an appetizer during one of their special holidays, or you can serve it with rice.

Duration: 1 hour 20 minutes

Serving Size: 25

List of Ingredients:

- 2 tbsp of sugar
- 1/2 tsp salt
- 1/2 cup of chili sauce
- 2 tbsp of cilantro, well chopped
- 1/2 cup of lime wedges for garnishing
- 1/2 cup of rice vinegar
- 1 cup of water
- 1 small red onion, well sliced
- 1 pack of frozen meatballs
- 2 tbsp of teriyaki sauce
- 1 tbsp of fish sauce
- 1 carrot, thinly sliced
- 1 tbsp of we'll sliced jalapeno
- 1/2 cup of mint, well chopped for garnishing

AAAAAAAAAAAAAAAAAAAAAAAA

Methods:

In a bowl, mix rice vinegar, water, salt, and sugar. Add onions to the mixture, cover the bowl, and refrigerate for at least 1 hour to pickle the onions.

Heat up a large pan and add the meatballs. Cook the meatballs until they turn brown, approximately 5 minutes. In a separate bowl, combine chili sauce, teriyaki sauce, and fish sauce, then pour the mixture over the meatballs in the pan. Cover the pan and cook for about 10 minutes.

Remove the cover from the pan and continue cooking and stirring the meatballs in the sauce until the sauce reaches the desired thickness.

Take the pan off the heat and add carrots, jalapeno, cilantro, and the pickled onions (from step 1). Garnish with mint and lime before serving the Meatball Sandwich while it's still warm.

Cooking Notes:

For the pickled onions, you can slice them thinly or dice them, depending on your preference. The longer they sit in the vinegar mixture, the more pronounced the pickled flavor will be.

When cooking the meatballs, ensure the pan is adequately preheated to get a nice sear on the meatballs and prevent them from sticking.

Adjust the cooking time for the meatballs based on their size. Cooking times may vary depending on whether they are homemade or store-bought.

Bread Selection: When choosing a roll or baguette for the Meatball Sandwich, opt for a sturdy one that can hold up well to the meatballs and toppings without getting soggy. A crusty French baguette or a hearty roll will work great.

Making Homemade Meatballs: If you prefer homemade meatballs, you can use ground beef, ground pork, or a combination of both. To enhance the flavors of the meatballs, consider adding minced garlic, grated ginger, chopped scallions, or a splash of soy sauce to the meatball mixture before shaping and cooking them.

Using Ground Chicken or Turkey: For a leaner option, you can use ground chicken or turkey instead of beef. Make sure to season the ground poultry with your desired herbs and spices to complement the flavors of the sauce.

Spicy Variation: To give the meatballs an extra kick, you can add chopped Thai bird chilies or crushed red pepper flakes to the sauce. Adjust the amount of spice according to your heat tolerance.

Vegetable Additions: Feel free to experiment with additional vegetables to add color and nutrition. Thinly sliced bell peppers, cucumber, or shredded cabbage are excellent choices to include in the sandwich.

Saucy Consistency: As the sauce thickens, be mindful not to overcook the meatballs, as they can become dry. Keep the sauce at a desired consistency that coats the meatballs nicely but retains some sauciness.

Meal Prep Option: You can make a large batch of meatballs and sauce ahead of time and store them separately in the refrigerator. When ready to serve, simply reheat the meatballs and sauce in a pan, add the pickled onions and garnishes, and assemble the sandwiches for a quick and delicious meal.

Serving Suggestion: To round out the meal, serve the Meatball Sandwich with a side of steamed rice, noodles, or a refreshing Asian-inspired slaw.

With these additional cooking notes, you can create a flavorful and customizable Meatball Sandwich that suits your taste preferences. Whether you prefer it spicier, milder, or packed with colorful vegetables, this sandwich offers a delightful blend of Asian-inspired flavors that will leave you satisfied and craving for more. Enjoy this delicious meal for a casual lunch, dinner, or even as a party appetizer!

15. Fried Crab Cakes and Aioli

Most people like to order this tasty crab cake from restaurants during the festive season; however, using our recipe, you will realize that it is tastier when it is homemade.

Duration: 40 minutes

Serving Size: 10

List of Ingredients:

- 15 oz of lump crab, drained
- 1/2 cup of breadcrumbs
- 1/2 tsp of ground black pepper
- 1 big egg, whisked lightly
- 1 tsp of white wine vinegar
- 1/3 tsp of cayenne pepper
- 1/2 cup of lemon wedges
- 2 tbsp of red bell pepper, well chopped
- 2 tbsp of green onions, well chopped
- 1/2 cup of mayonnaise, divided
- 2 tbsp of Dijon mustard
- 1 tbsp of oil
- 1 tsp of shallot, well minced

AAAAAAAAAAAAAAAAAAAAAAAA

Methods:

In a bowl, combine crab meat, onions, red pepper, part of the mayonnaise, part of the mustard, breadcrumbs, and pepper. Mix well, then add the eggs and mix thoroughly.

Use a measuring cup to portion the crab mixture into thick 1-inch cakes. Sprinkle a little oil on each cake.

Preheat your air fryer and grease the basket with a little oil. Place the crab cakes in the air fryer and cook for about 10 minutes or until they become crispy and golden. Repeat the process until all the crab cakes are cooked.

In another bowl, mix the remaining mayonnaise, shallots, vinegar, cayenne pepper, and mustard to create the aioli sauce.

Serve the fried crab cakes with the aioli sauce and lemon wedges for a delightful flavor combination.

Cooking Notes:

When mixing the crab cakes, be gentle to avoid breaking up the crab meat too much. It's best to have some chunky texture for a more enjoyable eating experience.

If you don't have an air fryer, you can also pan-fry the crab cakes in a skillet with a little oil over medium heat until they are golden and crispy on both sides.

Feel free to adjust the seasonings in the crab cake mixture according to your taste preferences. You can add more spices like Old Bay seasoning, garlic powder, or hot sauce for extra flavor.

Crab Meat Selection: When choosing crab meat for the crab cakes, you can opt for lump crab meat or claw meat, both of which work well for this recipe. You can also use a combination of both for a variety of textures.

Binding Agents: To help the crab cakes hold their shape, the eggs and breadcrumbs act as binding agents. If you prefer a gluten-free version, you can use gluten-free breadcrumbs or crushed rice crackers as a substitute.

Chilling the Crab Cakes: If you have the time, consider chilling the formed crab cakes in the refrigerator for about 30 minutes before air frying or pan-frying. Chilling helps the cakes firm up and hold their shape during cooking.

Aioli Variations: The aioli sauce can be customized to your liking. You can add a touch of sweetness with a teaspoon of honey or maple syrup, or make it tangier by adding a bit more vinegar or lemon juice. Adjust the amount of cayenne pepper for desired spiciness.

Breading the Crab Cakes: If you prefer a slightly crispier exterior, you can lightly coat the crab cakes in flour before air frying or pan-frying. The flour helps create a golden crust and locks in the moisture.

Make-Ahead Option: If you plan to prepare the crab cakes ahead of time, you can form them into cakes and store them in the refrigerator, covered, for a few hours or overnight. Cook them just before serving for a convenient and delicious treat.

Serving Suggestions: The crab cakes can be served as an appetizer, main course, or even as a filling for sandwiches or sliders. Pair them with a side salad, coleslaw, or roasted vegetables for a complete and satisfying meal.

Testing Doneness: To ensure the crab cakes are fully cooked, you can check the internal temperature using a meat thermometer. The internal temperature should reach 145°F (63°C) for cooked seafood.

With these additional cooking notes, you can confidently prepare scrumptious crab cakes with a delectable aioli sauce. This dish makes for an impressive appetizer or main course and is perfect for special occasions or casual gatherings with friends and family. Enjoy the crispy, flavorful crab cakes along with the zesty aioli sauce for a delightful and satisfying meal!

16. Halloween Cheddar Pumpkin Cheese Ball

When you mention Halloween, it can never be complete without this snack. When you shape your cheese balls into a pumpkin shape, it means the festive period is here, and kids need to have fun.

Duration: 2 hours 20 minutes

Serving Size: 30

List of Ingredients:

- 4 cups of crystal shredded cheddar cheese
- 1/3 tbsp of onion powder
- 1 tsp of dried mustard
- 1 tbsp of hot sauce
- 1/2 cup of pretzel sticks
- 1/2 cup of basil
- 1 pack of assorted crackers
- 3 packs of soft cream cheese
- 1/2 cup of cheddar cheese strips

AAAAAAAAAAAAAAAAAAAAAA

Methods:

In a bowl, mix cream cheese, cheddar cheese, mustard, hot sauce, and chopped onion together until well combined.

Lay out a plastic wrap and transfer the cheese mixture onto it. Wrap the mixture tightly to form a ball shape. Refrigerate it for at least 3 hours or until it becomes firm enough to shape.

Once the cheese mixture is chilled and firm, place it on a baking sheet. Use your hands to shape it into a pumpkin shape, creating ridges on the surface with your fingers.

Take cheese strips and place them into the ridges to resemble the pumpkin's segments. Add a pretzel at the top as the stem of the pumpkin. Optionally, you can use a basil leaf as a decorative leaf on the stem.

Serve the Halloween Cheddar Pumpkin Cheese Ball with your favorite crackers for a spooky and delicious treat!

Cooking Notes:

Feel free to adjust the amount of hot sauce used in the mixture according to your taste preferences. You can add more or less to achieve the desired level of spiciness.

For the cheese strips on the pumpkin, you can use thinly sliced cheddar cheese or other yellow cheese. You can also use a vegetable peeler to create long, thin strips from a block of cheese.

If you don't have hot sauce, you can use other spicy condiments like Sriracha or cayenne pepper to add some heat to the cheese mixture.

Cheese Variations: While the recipe calls for cream cheese and cheddar cheese, you can experiment with different types of cheeses to create unique flavor profiles. Try using gouda, pepper jack, or blue cheese for a more robust and distinct taste.

Enhancing Flavor: To add extra depth to the cheese ball, you can incorporate herbs and spices. Fresh or dried herbs like thyme, rosemary, or parsley can complement the cheese mixture beautifully. Additionally, a dash of garlic powder or onion powder can enhance the overall savory taste.

Personalizing the Pumpkin Shape: While shaping the cheese mixture, feel free to get creative with the pumpkin's appearance. You can create different patterns and textures on the surface, giving your cheese ball a more realistic or whimsical look, depending on the occasion.

Make-Ahead Option: The cheese ball can be made a day or two ahead of time and stored in the refrigerator until you're ready to serve it. Just keep it covered and tightly wrapped to retain freshness and prevent it from absorbing odors from the fridge.

Serving Presentation: To complete the Halloween theme, you can set the cheese ball on a decorative platter and surround it with crackers shaped like bats, ghosts, or pumpkins. You can also include a small sign next to the cheese ball with a spooky name like "Cheesy Jack-O-Lantern" for a fun touch.

Gluten-Free Option: If you want a gluten-free version, serve the cheese ball with gluten-free crackers or vegetable sticks, like carrot and celery sticks, for dipping.

Temperature Adjustment: Before serving, you can let the cheese ball sit at room temperature for a few minutes to soften slightly. This makes it easier for guests to spread the cheese on their crackers.

Multiple Cheese Balls: If you're serving a large group, consider making multiple smaller cheese balls instead of one large one. This allows for easy serving and encourages guests to gather around and enjoy the spooky appetizer.

With these additional cooking notes, you can create a delicious and eye-catching Halloween Cheddar Pumpkin Cheese Ball that will be a hit at your party or gathering. The combination of cheeses, spices, and decorative elements makes it a fun and tasty treat that everyone will enjoy. Happy Halloween!

17. Chocolate Chips and Crackers

A festive period cannot be complete without snacks. This is the perfect Halloween snack that you can make from the comfort of your home.

Duration: 10 minutes

Serving Size: 6

List of Ingredients:

- 2 tbsp of salted caramel
- 1/3 cup of chocolate chips, semi-sweet
- 20 pieces of Ritz crackers
- 2 apples, cut into 20 small pieces

AAAAAAAAAAAAAAAAAAAAAA

Methods:

Lay out the crackers on a serving platter or plate.

Place a slice of apple on top of each cracker.

Drizzle caramel topping over the apple slices.

Sprinkle chocolate chips on top of the caramel.

Serve the Chocolate Chips and Crackers as a delicious and easy-to-make snack.

Cooking Notes:

Choose crisp and sturdy crackers that can hold the toppings without breaking easily. You can use plain crackers or opt for flavored ones like graham crackers or butter crackers for added taste.

Select sweet and firm apple varieties that complement the chocolate and caramel flavors well. Popular choices include Honeycrisp, Fuji, or Pink Lady apples.

For the caramel topping, you can use store-bought caramel sauce or make your own by melting caramels with a bit of heavy cream for a homemade touch.

To enhance the flavors, you can sprinkle a pinch of sea salt or flaky salt over the caramel and chocolate chips. The saltiness balances the sweetness and adds a delightful contrast.

If you want to get creative, you can add other toppings like chopped nuts, shredded coconut, or drizzles of melted white chocolate or dark chocolate for a more indulgent treat.

Presentation: To make the Chocolate Chips and Crackers snack visually appealing, arrange the crackers in a neat pattern on the serving platter. You can create rows or a circular design to make it look more inviting.

Apple Slices: For a more eye-catching presentation, consider cutting the apple slices into different shapes, such as circles, triangles, or even using small cookie cutters to create fun shapes like stars or hearts.

Topping Variations: While the recipe calls for chocolate chips and caramel, you can experiment with various toppings to cater to different tastes. Try using peanut butter or almond butter as a spread instead of caramel for a nutty twist.

Drizzling Techniques: To achieve a more elegant look, use a small spoon or a squeeze bottle with a narrow tip to drizzle the caramel over the apple slices. This way, you can control the amount and create a decorative pattern.

Served with Ice Cream: For a delightful dessert option, you can serve the Chocolate Chips and Crackers alongside a scoop of vanilla ice cream. The combination of warm caramel and cold ice cream adds a lovely contrast of textures.

Party Platter: If you're preparing this snack for a party or gathering, consider setting up a toppings bar with various options. Guests can choose their favorite toppings and assemble their own personalized Chocolate Chips and Crackers.

Storage: Since the snack involves fresh apple slices, it's best served shortly after assembling to prevent browning. However, if you have leftovers, you can store the apple slices separately in an airtight container with a squeeze of lemon juice to maintain their color.

Dietary Modifications: If you have dietary restrictions or preferences, you can make this snack vegan-friendly by using dairy-free chocolate chips and caramel sauce. Additionally, gluten-free crackers can be used to accommodate those with gluten sensitivities.

By considering these additional cooking notes, you can create a delectable and visually appealing Chocolate Chips and Crackers snack that's perfect for any occasion. Whether it's a quick treat for yourself or a fun addition to a party spread, this sweet and crunchy snack is sure to be a hit. Enjoy!

18. Shrimp in Creamy Dip

This is very simple to make, and it is done occasionally. As the Christmas season is approaching, this is one meal you can't miss for anything.

Duration: 10 minutes

Serving Size: 15

List of Ingredients:

- 1 tbsp of lemon juice
- 1/2 tsp of cayenne pepper, ground
- 1/2 tbsp of paprika, smoked
- 1/3 tbsp of Worcestershire sauce
- 16 oz of softened cream cheese
- 1/2 cup of chili sauce
- 2 medium-sized well diced green onions
- 1 lb. of peeled, deveined, cooked, and chopped shrimp

AAAAAAAAAAAAAAAAAAAAAA

Methods:

In a bowl, combine lemon juice, chili sauce, cayenne pepper, cream cheese, paprika, and sauce to make the creamy dip.

Add green onions and shrimp to the creamy dip mixture, ensuring they are well coated.

Serve the Shrimp in Creamy Dip for a delicious and tangy appetizer.

Cooking Notes:

For the chili sauce, you can use any variety you prefer, such as Sriracha, sweet chili sauce, or a mild chili sauce, depending on your spice preference.

Adjust the amount of cayenne pepper according to how spicy you want the dip to be. Start with a small amount and gradually add more if desired.

Make sure the cream cheese is at room temperature or softened for easy mixing with the other ingredients.

Feel free to add additional seasonings or herbs to the creamy dip, such as garlic powder, chopped cilantro, or dill, to enhance the flavor.

Shrimp Options: When choosing shrimp for this recipe, consider using medium-sized or large shrimp. They are easier to handle and provide a more satisfying bite when dipped into the creamy sauce.

Shrimp Preparation: If you're using fresh shrimp, make sure to peel and devein them before adding them to the creamy dip. For frozen shrimp, thaw them completely and pat them dry with paper towels to remove excess moisture.

Dipping Alternatives: While crackers, bread slices, and vegetable sticks are great options for dipping, you can get creative with other dippable items. Try serving the creamy dip with tortilla chips, pita bread, or even crispy fried wonton wrappers for a unique twist.

Serving Bowls: Opt for a shallow serving bowl or a platter with raised edges to hold the creamy dip. This allows guests to easily dip their shrimp without making a mess.

Chilling Time: To enhance the flavors of the creamy dip and allow the ingredients to meld together, you can refrigerate the dip for about 30 minutes before serving. This also helps the dip thicken slightly for a better dipping consistency.

Party Platter: To create an impressive appetizer platter, arrange the Shrimp in Creamy Dip in the center of a large plate or serving tray. Surround the dip with an assortment of crackers, bread, and vegetables for a visually appealing presentation.

Dairy-Free Option: If you need a dairy-free version, you can substitute the cream cheese with a dairy-free cream cheese alternative or use a combination of silken tofu and vegan mayonnaise for a creamy texture.

Fresh Herbs: Adding chopped fresh herbs, such as parsley, chives, or basil, to the creamy dip can add a burst of freshness and complement the shrimp's flavors.

Customization: This recipe is versatile and can be adjusted to suit different tastes. Feel free to add diced bell peppers, minced garlic, or a splash of lemon zest for added complexity.

By incorporating these additional cooking notes, you can create a flavorful and versatile Shrimp in Creamy Dip that is sure to be a hit at any gathering. Whether it's a casual get-together or a more formal event, this appetizer provides a delightful balance of tangy and creamy flavors that pair perfectly with succulent shrimp. Enjoy!

19. Bread Pudding with Cinnamon Flavor

A festive period calls for special meals; however, make breakfast special by offering your family this delicious meal.

Duration: 70 minutes

Serving Size: 8

List of Ingredients:

- 1 loaf of cinnamon bread
- 2 cups of milk, low fat
- 2 cups of applesauce, unsweetened
- 1 tbsp of sugar
- 1 tbsp of cinnamon, ground
- 2 tbsp of butter cubes
- 1/2 can of cooking spray
- 1 can of caramel sauce
- 1 cup of raisins
- 2 well diced medium-sized apples
- 2 big eggs
- 1 tbsp of lemon zest

AAAAAAAAAAAAAAAAAAAAAAA

Methods:

Cut the bread into cube-sized pieces and spread them on a baking sheet. Allow the bread to dry overnight or for several hours.

Preheat your oven to 350° F (175° C). Grease a baking pan with cooking spray and set it aside.

In a bowl, mix the dried bread cubes, chopped apples, and raisins, and set the bowl aside.

In another bowl, whisk together the eggs, milk, sugar, applesauce, cinnamon, and lemon zest. Pour this mixture over the bread, apples, and raisins, and let it sit for about 15 minutes to allow the flavors to meld.

Transfer the bread mixture into the prepared baking pan. Top it with cubes of butter for added richness.

Bake the bread pudding in the preheated oven for approximately 45 minutes, or until it turns golden brown and is set in the center.

Once the bread pudding is done baking, remove it from the oven.

Serve the delicious Bread Pudding with Cinnamon Flavor warm and drizzle caramel sauce over each serving for a sweet and decadent touch.

Cooking Notes:

For the bread, you can use day-old bread or slightly stale bread for the best texture. The drying process helps the bread absorb the custard mixture better and prevents the pudding from becoming too soggy.

Experiment with different types of bread, such as brioche, challah, or French bread, to find your favorite flavor and texture combination.

For the apples, choose sweet and crisp varieties like Honeycrisp or Granny Smith for a delicious contrast to the creamy pudding.

Adjust the sweetness of the pudding by adding more or less sugar according to your taste preferences.

You can enhance the cinnamon flavor by using a mix of ground cinnamon and a small amount of freshly grated nutmeg.

While baking, keep an eye on the bread pudding to prevent it from overbrowning. If the top starts to get too dark, you can cover the pan loosely with aluminum foil.

Let the bread pudding rest for a few minutes before serving. It will continue to set as it cools slightly, making it easier to serve and enjoy.

20. Roasted Vegetable Salad

You are used to normal salads year in, year out, but this time you need something special and unique for the festive season, and we present this roasted salad to you to keep you excited all through the festive season.

Duration: 50 minutes

Serving Size: 6

List of Ingredients:

- 2 cups of Brussels Sprouts,
- 1 tsp of kosher salt
- 1/2 tsp of black pepper
- 2 tbsp of shallot, minced
- 1 tbsp of Dijon mustard
- 1 tbsp of maple syrup
- 2 tbsp of pecan, well chopped and toasted
- 1/2 cup of dried cherries
- 1/3 cup of pepitas
- 1/2 cup of oil
- 1 loaf of bread, cut in cube form
- 2 cups of butternut squash, cut in cube form
- 1 cup of apple cider
- 3 tbsp of apple cider vinegar
- 1 big well-diced apple
- 3 cups of kale

AAAAAAAAAAAAAAAAAAAAAAA

Methods:

Preheat your oven to 360° F (182° C). Line two baking pans with parchment paper. On one pan, place the bread cubes, and on the other pan, add the butternut squash and Brussels sprouts. Drizzle a little oil over them and season with salt and pepper. Mix until all the vegetables are well coated.

Place each pan in the preheated oven. Bake the bread cubes for about 10 minutes or until they become crispy and golden brown. Roast the Brussels sprouts and butternut squash for about 20 minutes or until they are tender.

In a small pan, add apple cider, shallots, and vinegar. Bring it to a boil, then reduce the heat and simmer for another 10 minutes. Remove the pan from the heat, pour the mixture into a glass, and add maple syrup, Dijon mustard, and oil to make the dressing.

In a large bowl, mix the roasted bread cubes, diced apples, kale, roasted Brussels sprouts and butternut squash, pecans, dried cherries, and pepitas.

Pour the cider dressing over the salad mixture and toss gently to combine all the ingredients.

Serve the delicious Roasted Vegetable Salad immediately and enjoy!

Cooking Notes:

Feel free to customize the vegetables according to your preference. You can use other seasonal vegetables like sweet potatoes, carrots, or cauliflower.

For added flavor, you can toss the vegetables in a mixture of olive oil, balsamic vinegar, and your favorite herbs or spices before roasting.

Adjust the roasting time based on the size and thickness of the vegetables. Smaller pieces may cook faster, so keep an eye on them to avoid overcooking.

To make the salad even heartier, you can add grilled chicken, cooked quinoa, or crumbled feta cheese.

For extra crunch, toast the pecans and pepitas in a dry skillet over medium heat for a few minutes until they become fragrant and slightly browned before adding them to the salad.

The cider dressing adds a tangy and slightly sweet taste to the salad. Feel free to adjust the sweetness by adding more or less maple syrup, depending on your preference.

Serve the salad while the roasted vegetables are still warm for a comforting and satisfying meal, or chill it in the refrigerator for a refreshing and nutritious cold salad option.

21. Black Bean and Chicken Enchilada

You want one meal to serve your family during the New Year celebration; this is perfect because the whole family will actually fall in love with it.

Duration: 20 minutes

Serving Size: 6

List of Ingredients:

- 1 medium sized onion, well diced
- 1 can of Rotel, which is a combination of diced tomatoes and green chilies
- 1 can of enchilada sauce
- 1/3 tbsp of cumin
- 1/3 tbsp of garlic powder
- 2 tbsp of oil
- 8 pieces of corn tortillas cut into strips
- 2 cups of boiled shredded chicken
- 1 clove of well-minced garlic
- 2 cans of black beans, nicely rinsed and drained
- 1 cup of cheddar cheese, shredded

AAAAAAAAAAAAAAAAAAAAAA

Methods:

In a pan, heat oil over medium heat. Add chicken, tortillas, onions, and garlic. Cook for about 5 minutes, stirring occasionally.

In another bowl, mix Rotel (diced tomatoes with green chilies), black beans, enchilada sauce, garlic powder, and cumin. Stir the mixture together and pour it over the chicken mixture in the pan.

Sprinkle part of the cheese on top of the mixture. Cover the pan and let it simmer for 5 minutes until the cheese melts and the flavors blend.

Remove the pan from heat and serve the delicious Black Bean and Chicken Enchilada. Top each serving with the remaining cheese for added creaminess and flavor.

Cooking Notes:

For the chicken, you can use cooked and shredded chicken breasts or thighs. You can also use rotisserie chicken for a quick and easy option.

When sautéing the chicken, onions, and garlic, you can add some seasoning like salt, pepper, and chili powder for extra flavor.

Use corn tortillas for a gluten-free version, or flour tortillas if you prefer their taste and texture.

If you prefer a spicier enchilada, you can use hot Rotel or add some diced jalapenos or green chilies to the mixture.

Customize the enchilada sauce according to your taste preference. You can use red or green enchilada sauce, or a mix of both, depending on your desired level of spiciness and flavor.

Feel free to add other ingredients to the filling, such as bell peppers, corn, or spinach, to make the dish more nutritious and colorful.

For a creamier enchilada, you can mix some sour cream or cream cheese into the sauce before pouring it over the chicken mixture.

Garnish the enchiladas with fresh cilantro, diced tomatoes, avocado slices, or a dollop of sour cream for a beautiful presentation and added freshness.

22. Shrimp and Cheese

What is a better way to impress your guests during a festive period than treating them to a wonderful Shrimp and Cheese?

Duration: 40 minutes

Serving Size: 16

List of Ingredients:

- 1 lb. cooked, deveined, and peeled shrimp
- 1/2 can of crumbled cheese
- 1/2 cup of balsamic glaze
- 1 loaf of French bread
- 1/2 cup of oil
- 1/3 cup of pesto
- 1/2 cup of sun-dried tomatoes

AAAAAAAAAAAAAAAAAAAAAA

Methods:

Preheat your oven to 380° F (193° C).

Slice the bread and brush both sides with oil. Place the bread slices on a baking sheet and bake until they become golden brown on both sides. Allow them to cool for about 5 minutes.

Spread pesto sauce on each bread slice. Top them with sliced tomatoes, cheese, and cooked shrimp. Finish by sprinkling balsamic glaze over the toppings.

Serve the delicious Shrimp and Cheese appetizers immediately for a flavorful and satisfying treat.

Cooking Notes:

Choose a crusty bread like baguette or ciabatta for the best texture and ability to hold the toppings without becoming too soggy.

You can use store-bought pesto or make your own by blending fresh basil, garlic, pine nuts, Parmesan cheese, and olive oil.

For the tomatoes, use ripe and juicy tomatoes like Roma or cherry tomatoes for a burst of freshness.

Feel free to experiment with different types of cheese. Mozzarella, feta, or goat cheese work well in this recipe.

To cook the shrimp, you can sauté them in a pan with a little oil and seasoning until they turn pink and opaque. Alternatively, you can use pre-cooked shrimp for convenience.

Balsamic glaze adds a tangy and slightly sweet flavor to the appetizers. You can find it at most grocery stores or make your own by reducing balsamic vinegar until it thickens into a syrup-like consistency.

For added flavor and texture, you can add some fresh basil leaves, arugula, or microgreens on top of the toppings before serving.

Serve the Shrimp and Cheese appetizers as an impressive and delightful option for parties, gatherings, or as a light meal. They are easy to assemble and can be prepared in advance, making them perfect for entertaining.

23. Grilled Cheese and Avocado

You don't necessarily need to prepare a heavy meal all the time; this is one snack that can be taken in between meals because a festive period is a time when people eat, rest and have fun.

Duration: 10 minutes

Serving Size: 6

List of Ingredients:

- 2 bell of well-sliced Roma tomatoes
- 1 avocado, cut into 9 pieces
- 3 pieces of pepper jack cheese cut into 6
- 18 pieces of crackers Triscuit

AAAAAAAAAAAAAAAAAAAAAAA

Methods:

Preheat your oven to 350° F (175° C).

Arrange the crackers on a baking sheet in a single layer.

Top each cracker with slices of tomatoes, avocado, and cheese.

Bake the assembled crackers in the preheated oven until the cheese melts and becomes bubbly.

Remove the baking sheet from the oven and serve the delicious Grilled Cheese and Avocado appetizers.

Cooking Notes:

Choose sturdy crackers that can hold the toppings without becoming too soggy during baking. You can use plain or flavored crackers, depending on your preference.

For the tomatoes, use ripe and juicy tomatoes for the best flavor and texture.

Use ripe avocados that are firm yet slightly soft to the touch. Slice them thinly for easier assembly and better distribution on the crackers.

Select your favorite type of cheese for this recipe. Cheddar, mozzarella, pepper jack, or Swiss are popular choices that pair well with the other ingredients.

Feel free to add some seasoning to enhance the flavors. A pinch of salt, pepper, or dried herbs like basil or oregano can add extra taste to the appetizers.

Alternatively, you can use a toaster oven or broiler to melt the cheese quickly if you prefer not to use the oven.

For added texture and flavor, you can sprinkle some toasted pine nuts, sunflower seeds, or sesame seeds on top of the avocado and cheese before baking.

Serve the Grilled Cheese and Avocado appetizers immediately while they are still warm for a tasty and easy-to-make snack or party treat.

24. Chicken and Tortilla Soup

The Christmas period is always cold, and serving the soul will be a perfect way to start the day, and the best part is it is easy and quick to prepare.

Duration: 30 minutes

Serving Size: 5

List of Ingredients:

- 2 tbsp of oil
- 4 cups of unsalted chicken broth
- 1/2 tsp of salt
- 1/3 tsp of black pepper
- 1 cup of tortilla chips well crushed
- 1/2 cup of cilantro, well chopped
- 2 cans of chicken breast, boneless, skinless, and shredded
- 2 cups of yellow onions, well chopped
- 1 cup of carrot, well chopped
- 1 well chopped poblano pepper
- 1 can of diced tomatoes

AAAAAAAAAAAAAAAAAAAAAA

Methods:

In a pan, heat oil over medium heat. Add onions, poblano, and carrot. Sauté for about 10 minutes, stirring frequently, until the vegetables become tender.

Pour in the chicken broth, add pepper, salt, and tomatoes to the pan. Stir everything together and allow it to come to a boil.

Crush tortilla chips and add them to the boiling mixture. Cover the pan and let it simmer until the carrot is fully tender. Then, add cooked chicken and cilantro to the soup.

Ladle the Chicken and Tortilla Soup into individual soup bowls and serve it hot.

Cooking Notes:

For the onions, poblano, and carrots, chop them into small, uniform pieces to ensure even cooking and a better texture in the soup.

You can use pre-cooked and shredded chicken breasts or thighs for convenience. Rotisserie chicken is also a great option.

For added flavor, you can season the soup with spices like cumin, paprika, or chili powder, depending on your taste preferences.

The crushed tortilla chips will add a nice thickness and corn flavor to the soup. You can also use store-bought tortilla strips or strips made from tortillas.

For a heartier soup, you can add black beans or corn kernels along with the chicken and cilantro.

If you prefer a spicier version, you can add diced jalapenos or red pepper flakes to the soup while sautéing the vegetables.

Garnish the soup with additional cilantro, diced avocado, shredded cheese, or a squeeze of lime juice for added freshness and appeal.

This soup can be easily customized to suit your taste preferences. Feel free to experiment with different vegetables, spices, or toppings to create your perfect Chicken and Tortilla Soup.

25. Goat Cheese and Wrapped Bacon and Dates

With bacon, you can say everything is better; however, when it comes to festive periods and throwing parties, wrapped bacon and goat cheese tastes even better.

Duration: 30 minutes

Serving Size: 15

List of Ingredients:

- 5 oz of goat cheese
- 1 pack of toothpick
- 7 slices of festival bacon
- 15 dates

AAAAAAAAAAAAAAAAAAAAAA

Methods:

Preheat your oven to 350° F (175° C).

Slice the dates and create an opening, then remove the pit from each date. Stuff a small amount of goat cheese into the middle of each date and close it up.

Cut the bacon slices in half and wrap each date with one slice of bacon. Use a toothpick to secure the bacon-wrapped dates. Arrange them properly on a baking sheet with raised edges to catch any dripping bacon grease.

Bake the bacon-wrapped dates in the preheated oven for about 10 minutes. After that, remove the dates from the oven, carefully turn them to the other side, and bake for another 10 minutes or until the bacon becomes brown and crispy, depending on your preference.

Remove the bacon-wrapped dates from the oven and drain them on a paper towel to remove any excess grease.

Serve the delicious Goat Cheese and Wrapped Bacon and Dates as a delightful and savory appetizer.

Cooking Notes:

Choose soft and moist dates for this recipe, such as Medjool dates, as they will provide a nice contrast to the crispy bacon and creamy goat cheese.

Feel free to add some chopped nuts like almonds or pecans to the goat cheese filling for added texture and nutty flavor.

When wrapping the bacon around the dates, make sure to wrap it tightly, but not too tight to avoid squeezing out the goat cheese filling.

For a touch of sweetness, you can drizzle honey or maple syrup over the bacon-wrapped dates before baking.

As an optional step, you can sprinkle some black pepper or smoked paprika over the bacon-wrapped dates for additional flavor.

The bacon-wrapped dates can be served on their own or with a side of dipping sauce like balsamic glaze, barbecue sauce, or a spicy aioli for added taste.

Make sure to remove the toothpicks before serving to prevent any accidental swallowing. You can also use decorative toothpicks or cocktail sticks for an attractive presentation.

These appetizers are perfect for parties, gatherings, or as a delicious finger food option. They are quick and easy to make and will surely be a hit among your guests.

26. Meatballs in Barbeque Sauce and Beer

What a way to enjoy a nice appetizer! This combination is amazing, and everyone will love it.

Duration: 3 hours

Serving Size: 20

List of Ingredients:

- 1 cup of beer
- 1 pack of frozen meatballs
- 1 can of barbeque sauce

AAAAAAAAAAAAAAAAAAAAA

Methods:

Place the meatballs in a slow cooker.

Pour the barbeque sauce and beer over the meatballs. Stir everything together to ensure the meatballs are coated with the sauce and beer.

Cook the meatballs on a low setting in the slow cooker for 3 hours. Stir the mixture often during the cooking process to prevent sticking and ensure even cooking.

After 3 hours, remove the meatballs from the slow cooker and serve them warm.

Cooking Notes:

Use your favorite brand of barbeque sauce for this recipe. You can opt for a sweet and smoky flavor or a tangy and spicy one, depending on your taste preferences.

Choose a beer that compliments the flavor of the barbeque sauce. A lager, ale, or even a stout can add depth and richness to the dish.

For the meatballs, you can use pre-made frozen meatballs for convenience or make your own using ground beef, pork, or a mixture of both.

To enhance the flavor of the meatballs, you can season them with garlic powder, onion powder, salt, and pepper before placing them in the slow cooker.

Stirring the meatballs and sauce often during the slow cooking process will help distribute the flavors and prevent the sauce from burning or sticking to the sides of the slow cooker.

Serve the meatballs as an appetizer or as a main dish. They can be enjoyed on their own or served with sides like mashed potatoes, coleslaw, or cornbread.

If you prefer a thicker sauce, you can mix some cornstarch with water and stir it into the sauce during the last 30 minutes of cooking to thicken it up.

Garnish the meatballs with chopped fresh parsley or green onions for a pop of color and freshness before serving.

These meatballs are perfect for parties, potlucks, or weeknight dinners. They are easy to make, and the slow cooking process allows the flavors to meld together, resulting in tender and flavorful meatballs.

27. Mixed Rice Bowl

This is another special Korean meal that is often called bibimbap. It's a combination of vegetables, rice, eggs, etc. It is the perfect festive meal.

Duration: 25 minutes

Serving Size: 4

List of Ingredients:

- 2 tsp of sesame oil
- 1/2 cup of bean sprout
- 1 cup of carrot, shredded
- 1 pack of mushrooms well sliced
- 2 cups of spinach
- 2 cups of brown rice already cooked
- 4 poached eggs
- 2 cloves of well minced garlic
- 1 lb. ground sirloin
- 1/2 cup of water

AAAAAAAAAAAAAAAAAAAAAAA

Methods:

Heat 1 tsp of sesame oil in a pan. Add some garlic and simmer for 1 minute.

Add the sirloin to the pan and cook until it is browned. Set the cooked sirloin aside.

In another pan, heat a little sesame oil and add the bean sprouts and carrots. Fry them for about 5 minutes. Remove them from the pan and set aside.

In the same pan, add the remaining sesame oil and more garlic. Fry the mushrooms for 5 minutes. Then, add a little water and the spinach to the pan and cook until the spinach wilts. Remove from heat and set aside.

Divide the rice into 4 bowls.

Top each bowl of rice with the cooked sirloin, bean sprouts, carrots, spinach, and mushrooms.

Add a poached egg to each bowl.

Serve the delicious Mixed Rice Bowl immediately, and enjoy!

Cooking Notes:

For the best flavor, use toasted sesame oil. It has a nutty and rich taste that enhances the overall dish.

Make sure to cook the sirloin until it reaches your desired level of doneness. You can cook it medium-rare or well-done, depending on your preference.

When frying the bean sprouts and carrots, stir them often to ensure even cooking and prevent them from sticking to the pan.

The mushrooms release moisture when cooked, which is why they are fried without water initially. Once they are slightly caramelized, a little water is added to prevent them from drying out and to create a flavorful sauce.

To poach eggs, bring a pot of water to a gentle simmer, add a splash of vinegar, and create a gentle whirlpool in the water. Crack an egg into the center of the whirlpool and cook for about 3-4 minutes until the white is set, but the yolk is still runny.

You can add some sauce or dressing of your choice to the rice bowl for extra flavor. Teriyaki sauce, soy sauce, or a sesame ginger dressing are excellent options.

Customize the ingredients to your liking. You can add sliced avocado, shredded seaweed, or pickled vegetables for additional taste and texture.

The Mixed Rice Bowl is a balanced and nutritious meal with protein from the beef and egg, fiber from the vegetables, and carbohydrates from the rice. Enjoy it as a satisfying and healthy lunch or dinner option.

28. Stuffing in a Traditional Way

This meal is a must for the forthcoming festive season, and you can't miss it for anything. It is classy and unique.

Duration: 2 hours 20 minutes

Serving Size: 6

List of Ingredients:

- 1 loaf of French bread
- 6 stalks of diced celery
- 1/3 cup of Italian parsley, well minced
- 3 tbsp of minced rosemary leaves
- 1/2 cup of minced fresh thyme leaves
- 2 cups of chicken broth, shared in two parts
- 1/2 tsp of pepper
- 2 big eggs
- 2 tbsp of butter
- 1 big yellow onion, well diced
- 1/2 cup of minced sage leaves
- 1 tsp of salt

AAAAAAAAAAAAAAAAAAAAAA

Methods:

Preheat your oven to 240° F (115° C).

Cut the bread into cubes and spread them on a baking sheet. Bake the bread cubes for about 45 minutes, stirring often to ensure even toasting. Transfer the toasted bread cubes to a large bowl.

Increase the oven temperature to 300° F (150° C) and grease a baking pan. In a large pan, melt the butter over medium heat. Add the onions and celery, and sauté for about 10 minutes until they become soft and translucent. Transfer the sautéed onions and celery to the bowl with the bread cubes.

Add the parsley, sage, thyme, rosemary, part of the chicken broth, salt, and pepper to the bowl with the bread mixture. Toss everything together to combine, and set it aside.

In another bowl, mix the remaining chicken broth and eggs together. Pour the mixture over the bread mixture in the large bowl and toss everything together to ensure the bread is evenly moistened.

Transfer the stuffing mixture to the greased baking dish and cover it with foil.

Bake the stuffing in the preheated oven for 40 minutes. Then, remove the foil and continue baking for another 40 minutes or until the top becomes golden brown and crispy.

Remove the stuffing from the oven and serve it as a delicious and classic side dish for your holiday meals or any special occasion.

Cooking Notes:

For the bread, you can use stale or slightly dried-out bread, as it will absorb the flavors and moisture better during baking. You can also use a mix of different types of bread, like white, whole wheat, or cornbread, for added depth of flavor.

When toasting the bread cubes, keep an eye on them and stir frequently to prevent them from burning. Toasting the bread will help enhance its flavor and texture in the stuffing.

The mixture of herbs (parsley, sage, thyme, and rosemary) adds a traditional and savory flavor to the stuffing. You can adjust the amount of herbs to suit your taste preferences.

The chicken broth and eggs serve as the binding agent for the stuffing. The eggs will help hold the ingredients together and add moisture to the dish during baking.

You can customize the stuffing by adding other ingredients like diced apples, dried cranberries, chopped nuts, or cooked sausage for extra taste and texture.

Stuffing can be made in advance and refrigerated until ready to bake. When ready to serve, bring it to room temperature before baking.

This stuffing pairs well with roast turkey, chicken, pork, or as a vegetarian side dish. It's a comforting and flavorful addition to any festive meal.

29. Creamy Avocado Chocolate Pudding

Using your creamy avocado, this chocolate pudding will be the best dessert your family will have during a festive period.

Duration: 3 hours 10 minutes

Serving Size: 6

List of Ingredients:

- 1/2 cup of chocolate milk, low fat preferable
- 1/3 tsp of ground cinnamon
- 1/3 tsp of sea salt
- 1/3 cup of raspberries
- 1/2 cup of dark chocolate chips, nicely melted
- 2 ripe peeled and pitted avocados
- 1/2 cup of maple syrup
- 1/2 tbsp of vanilla extract

AAAAAAAAAAAAAAAAAAAAAA

Methods:

Melt the dark chocolate chips in the microwave, stirring until completely melted. Let it sit for about 2 minutes to cool slightly.

In a food processor, combine the melted dark chocolate, maple syrup, vanilla extract, chocolate milk, cinnamon, and salt. Blend everything together until the mixture becomes smooth and creamy.

Transfer the creamy avocado chocolate pudding to a jar and refrigerate it for at least 3 hours to chill and set.

Serve the chilled avocado chocolate pudding with fresh raspberries for a delightful and indulgent treat.

Cooking Notes:

Use good quality dark chocolate chips for the best flavor. The higher the cocoa content, the richer and more intense the chocolate flavor will be.

If you prefer a sweeter pudding, you can adjust the amount of maple syrup to your taste. You can also use other sweeteners like honey or agave syrup.

To make the pudding even creamier, you can add a splash of heavy cream or coconut cream during blending.

Cinnamon adds a warm and aromatic touch to the pudding, but you can omit it if you're not a fan of cinnamon or prefer a more straightforward chocolate flavor.

Ensure that the melted chocolate has cooled slightly before blending it with the other ingredients to avoid curdling or cooking the avocado.

If you want a smoother texture, you can strain the pudding mixture through a fine-mesh sieve after blending to remove any lumps or avocado fibers.

For a thicker pudding, you can add some chia seeds or gelatin while blending. This will also make it more suitable for layering in a parfait or using as a filling for cakes and pastries.

The pudding can be stored in the refrigerator for a couple of days, but it is best to consume it within 2-3 days for the freshest taste and texture.

Feel free to garnish the creamy avocado chocolate pudding with other toppings like shredded coconut, chopped nuts, or a dollop of whipped cream for added flavor and presentation.

Avocado adds a creamy and nutritious twist to traditional chocolate pudding, providing healthy fats and a velvety texture. Enjoy this guilt-free dessert as a delicious and satisfying treat.

30. Lemon Seed Cake and Raspberries

New Year celebration is supposed to be fun all through, and even the snacks and meals should also be fun. Try this, and thank us later.

Duration: 20 minutes

Serving Size: 16

List of Ingredients:

- 1 can of frozen whip
- 2 loaves of lemon seed cake, cut in cube size
- 3 cans of raspberries
- 1 lemon, well sliced
- 1 cup of condensed milk
- 2 cups of low-fat milk
- 1 pack of cheesecake pudding

AAAAAAAAAAAAAAAAAAAAAA

Methods:

In a bowl, combine the condensed milk, low-fat milk, and pudding mix. Mix everything together and let it sit for 5 minutes to allow the pudding to set. Gently fold in the frozen whipped topping to make the creamy pudding mixture.

Begin layering the trifle dish with slices of lemon seed cake. Pour a portion of the pudding mixture over the cake layer. Add some raspberries on top of the pudding layer.

Repeat the layering process with another layer of lemon seed cake, pudding mixture, and raspberries. Continue until the trifle dish is filled, ending with a layer of raspberries on top.

Garnish the top of the trifle with lemon slices and more raspberries for a fresh and vibrant appearance.

You can serve the lemon seed cake trifle immediately after assembling it, or for an even better taste, chill it in the fridge for a few hours before serving. Chilling allows the flavors to meld together and creates a more cohesive and delicious dessert.

Cooking Notes:

Lemon seed cake is a flavorful and moist cake that pairs wonderfully with the creamy pudding and tart raspberries in this trifle. However, you can use any other cake of your choice, such as pound cake or sponge cake, if lemon seed cake is not available.

To enhance the lemon flavor, you can drizzle some lemon syrup or lemon juice over the cake layers before adding the pudding mixture.

The pudding mixture can be prepared with various flavors, like vanilla, chocolate, or coconut, depending on your preference. Experiment with different pudding flavors to create unique and tasty variations of the trifle.

Fresh raspberries are preferable for this recipe, but you can also use frozen raspberries if fresh ones are not available. Just make sure to thaw and drain the frozen raspberries before using them in the trifle.

If you want to add more texture to the trifle, you can sprinkle some toasted sliced almonds or chopped pistachios between the cake and pudding layers.

Trifles are very forgiving desserts, and you can adjust the quantities of the ingredients according to your taste and the size of your trifle dish.

Trifles are best served chilled, as the flavors meld together and the layers set nicely. The dessert can be prepared in advance, making it a convenient option for parties and gatherings.

As a finishing touch, you can dust the top of the trifle with a little powdered sugar or drizzle it with a light lemon glaze for added sweetness and decoration. Enjoy the delightful combination of lemony cake, creamy pudding, and tangy raspberries in this refreshing dessert.

See You Again

Thank you for purchasing and reading my book. Your support means a lot, and I'm grateful you chose my book among many options. I write to help people like you, who appreciate every word.

Please share your thoughts on the book, as reader feedback helps me grow and improve. Your insights may even inspire others. Thanks again!

Printed in Great Britain
by Amazon

HOW TO GO VEGAN

A guide to becoming vegan for normal people

Francesca Dixon-Grant

DISCLAIMER

This book was written with the intention to provide information and motivation to readers who are interested in becoming vegan. This book is not to be used to diagnose or treat any medical conditions. The author and publisher shall not be liable for any physical, psychological, emotional or finanical damages. You should consult your GP before making any changes to your diet. The content of this book is the opinion of the author, who is not a medical professional. References, where provided are for informative purposes only and don't constitue endorsement of other people, content or services. You, as the reader, are responsible for your own actions, choices and results.

CONTENTS

INTRODUCTION

Hello and welcome to the beautiful world of veganism! Before I start to unleash the secrets of simple vegan-eating, I want to give you a bit of a background about who I am and why I decided to write this book.

I have been a vegan for two years at the time of writing this book. I enjoy cycling, geocaching, yoga and walks with my husband and dog. I also enjoy eating food and lots of it! Which is why my family was so shocked when I turned vegan. When I say I loved food, I literally mean that I would have takeaway every week and that my idea of cooking a meal was to chuck some frozen chicken dippers and potato waffles in an oven and maybe even a frozen pizza too if I was particularly hungry. I remember when I once diced up a chicken breast for the first time, fried it off and added it to a tin of tomato soup as a 'healthy' dinner – I honestly thought I had created a gourmet meal! It got to the point where, if someone was giving me directions, they would describe where to go by naming fast-food locations that were nearby my destination as I was sure to know where all of the surrounding fast-food outlets were! In the course of a month, I would normally have at least five different types of takeaway from both major fast-food outlets and my local takeaways. When I was growing up, if someone in my household didn't finish their dinner, the remains would be offered to me first before binning it and, nine times out of ten, I would polish them off. I also loved chocolate. A bit too much. You know those enormous bars of chocolate you can buy at Christmas-time? Yeah, I could eat an entire one of those in just one sitting.

You might be wondering why I'm telling you all of this! It's because I want to show the world that if a self-proclaimed fast food, frozen food and choc-oholic like I was can make the change to go vegan, then ANYONE can do it if you truly want to.

And that is exactly why I have written this book. When I first went vegan, I found it quite hard to know what to eat and lived on pasta for a while whilst I figured out what else I could eat. At the time, I didn't have any other close friends who were vegan and my only vegan family member lived in Australia – so they weren't exactly just down the road for me to bombard with questions. So it really was a case of making it up as I went along.

I used to spend hours and hours in the evenings, scouring the internet for 'easy vegan recipes', 'recipes for beginner vegans', 'simple easy vegan meals' and any other different combinations of those words and their synonyms that you can possibly think of! What I found was that recipe, after recipe, after recipe, I would just be confronted with crazy-long ingredient lists that surely only a trained chef was supposed to be able to understand and cooking methods that, for me, someone who could rarely cook oven-food without burning it, found way too complicated. So, it was a bit disheartening to say the least! Finally, I managed to find about five recipes that I thought I could understand and would just rotate these around for dinner on a weekly basis. Unfortunately, this soon started to get a bit boring and off I went again on the search for new recipes, hoping that this time, I would be able to understand them... No chance.

Then I discovered the world of vegan social media and boy, was

I relieved! This time I thought I would definitely be able to find something I could cook so, again, I spent hours upon hours scrolling through the hundreds of glamorous photos of vegan meals, getting rather hungry in the process! What did I learn? That there are some amazing people out there who can create the most incredible-looking vegan meals and then take an even more incredible photo of them. But, there STILL didn't seem to be anything that a normal person (i.e. me – not very good at cooking and definitely not anywhere near to being a chef) would be able to copy and make themselves. Like seriously, even now I can't even pronounce half of the ingredients that I see on these recipes, let alone be able to identify any of them in a supermarket. Now I was getting fed-up.

Which brings me to why I decided to write this book! I may not have been a vegan all my life, I can't name all of the herbs and spices under the sun, I am certainly not a chef and would struggle to produce an Instagram-worthy dinner BUT I do love food and I love being vegan even more than I love food. What I wanted to do in this book is to give all of you aspiring-vegans and beginner-vegans – who, like me, unfortunately weren't born with culinary superpowers – the tools to become a vegan and to make your journey to veganism much easier. Being vegan is an amazing, wonderful thing and has many incredible benefits both for your personal health and for our environment and so if I can help at least one person to make the transition to a heathier lifestyle, then I will be happy.

I really do hope you enjoy this book and the amazing vegan adventure that lies ahead of you!

1. WHY IT SEEMS SCARY GOING VEGAN

L et's be honest, we've all had a time in our lives when we've thought that people who follow a vegan diet must be completely mad.

"So they can't eat chocolate, or pizza, or cheese?! I couldn't live without cheese!"

And I'm sure many of us have asked a vegan the famous question: *"But what do you actually eat?!"* I remember practically shouting that question at a friend of my husband's in a not-so-subtle attempt to try and get my confused brain around what seemed to be, at the time, an absolutely impossible feat of superhuman willpower and mental strength. I mean, I honestly, literally couldn't, at that time, think of anything that a vegan would be able to eat apart from fruit and vegetables.

So there lies our first big problem – lack of knowledge.

Lack Of Knowledge

I can absolutely say that it wasn't until I actually made the decision to become a vegan and started eating a vegan diet that

I learnt about the different foods that I could eat. Sometimes I guess you just have to jump right in at the deep-end and for me this was one of those times. But I can also say that, miraculously, I didn't starve to death and I did actually find something else to eat other than beans. (That's another fun question I've been asked before: "What do you eat, just beans?" to which I like to simply answer "Yep, that's it" just for the fun of seeing their confused expression afterwards!) In fact, quite on the contrary, I always seem to find plenty to eat!

When you think about it, if you haven't been vegan since childhood then going vegan for the first time is a huge change. Not only to your diet but to your lifestyle too because it's not just the food you eat that it affects. For example, think about how it affects your shopping habits: you have to start studying labels, finding aisles in the supermarket that you would usually avoid and probably even purchasing food that you've never even heard of before. But even more of a change is the change to your thought-processes about food. If, all of your life, you have grown up being taught that animal products are good for you and including some sort of animal product in every meal – cow's milk on cereal for breakfast, chicken and cheese sandwich for lunch, followed by pork chops for dinner – then suddenly not including any of these products in your diet any more can be a huge shock to the system initially. Trying to plan meals without these products can seem near impossible to begin with, but I promise you that it gets easier.

So, lack of knowledge about things like what food to eat, how to read labels, how to shop for vegan food, what to eat if you go out for a meal, can all easily affect someone's decision to go vegan or not and I think is probably the single biggest reason why people don't make the decision to go vegan. But don't worry! This beautiful little book is here to teach you about all of the foods that you can actually eat as a vegan and will make the lack-of-knowledge-phase a LOT easier.

Social Support

The second main problem that I think people face when considering becoming vegan is a lack of social support. Now, by this, I don't just mean that people are going to be constantly trying to wave chicken drumsticks in your face or smugly asking if you're sure you don't want one teeny, tiny piece of cheese because cheese never killed anybody... yeah right. I am talking about all sorts of social situations and relationships which may play a factor in your decision to go vegan. I'm sure that you have probably worried at least once about what other people might say or think when you tell them that you're vegan for the first time.

Just imagine it now, you turn up to your Nanna's house on boxing day for a Christmas celebration and your whole family are there. Nanna has set out an enormous spread of food on the kitchen table and there are bowls of snacks everywhere the eye can see throughout the room. Seconds after wishing everyone a Merry Christmas and finding a spare patch of carpet or corner of an armchair to sit on, a plate of 'your favourite' food, which Nanna has spent all day in the kitchen slaving over, is thrust into your hand under an expectant eye that you eat and enjoy it. Well, here it goes, this is the moment you've been dreading – "Oh, no, that's ok thank you, I won't be able to eat any of it, because I'm vegan now... it looks delicious though." Silence throughout the room. Crickets. All eyes turned your way. "You're what?!" your shocked mother asks from across the room: "But you love chocolate!". "And cheese!" "And pizza" – everyone starts piping up now, listing food that you will no longer be able to eat and how you must have gone crazy, insisting that it won't last long. You try to find your confident only-two-weeks-as-a-vegan voice and begin to carefully explain some of those well-prepared reasons that you had been rehearsing in the car on the drive over with your husband, but they don't come out how you planned them to and soon an almost-argument has broken out across the room about how dairy is good for you and gives you strong bones and all you can do is listen quietly when your family of suddenly-fully-qualified-doctors begins telling you about all the ways that you will become unhealthy when you go vegan. Whilst your poor Nanna, still holding the plate of refused food in her hand, looks around completely bemused as if you've suddenly sprouted wings and started tap-dancing naked on her perfectly-polished brass ornaments.

If you haven't gathered – that delightful little story above is what happened to me when I finally had to admit to my family that I had turned vegan. Their takeaway-loving, cheese-adoring, chocolate-guzzling daughter had lost the plot. That story, I think, is a perfect example of how a lack of social support could easily be enough to put someone off becoming a vegan for the first time. It can be difficult to face up to friends and family that know you well (and have known you well as an animal-eater) and the barrage of questions that they undeniably will have about you becoming vegan. Unfortunately though, I think this is probably a part of turning vegan that most new vegans will have to endure. But don't despair! This initial outrage and confusion phase doesn't tend to last long and, before you know it, your family and friends will be sending you links to vegan recipes and photos of vegan food that they've seen in supermarkets and vegan cafés that they have spotted which you should visit. It is hard to step away from 'the norm' and especially from the way that you have been raised, but believe me friends, it is worthwhile.

Other social situations that may feel a bit awkward or take some readjusting to at the beginning can include things like: shared food in the staff room (which there is a lot of if you are a teacher!),

Christmas-dos, meals-out with friends and other situations in-volving other people. These sorts of situations open you up to questions about why you're not eating (for example if there's non-vegan food available and people don't yet know that you're vegan) or more direct questions about why exactly you decided to go vegan. Now, please don't think I am trying to scare you into being worried about any possible interactions that you may have with other human-beings about your dietary choices. People are curious creatures and it is only natural that they will ask you questions. I find, a lot of the time, people are just genuinely inter-ested in how I manage being a vegan and actually, a lot of conver-sations tend to centre around the positive benefits of veganism. More than once I have had meat-eaters say to me, "I wish I could be vegan, but I just couldn't give up... [inset cheese, steak, eggs or various other animal products here]". Use these opportunities to spread your love of being vegan and the wonderful, healthful way that it makes you feel. Be confident in your decision to change your diet and life for the better and don't worry about what any-one else thinks about it.

Lack Of Confidence

Which brings us to the last issue: lack of confidence. This could incorporate the first two problems; a lack of confidence about what to eat, or a lack of confidence about how you would ap-proach any questions asked of you in social situations. But what I am mainly referring to when I talk about a lack of confidence is actually a lack of confidence in yourself.

I wanted to go vegan for months before I actually decide to 'take the leap' and do it. I watched lots of programmes, including the mind-blowing "What the Health?" and the brilliant "Forks over Knives" on Netflix – massive shout out to you guys for the inspir-ation – looked up lots of recipes and talked about it A LOT with my husband. In the end, after having been vegetarian for a few months, we decided that a gradual approach wasn't going to work for us and decided that we were going to turn vegan the very next day. Admittedly, this day did turn into a week as we worked our way through all of the vegetarian-but-not-vegan food that we had left in the freezer but we still did it and neither of us have ever regretted our decision. We love being vegan.

But it wasn't an easy decision. Like I said, it took us months to actually make the decision to make the change and the main reason for this was because we thought that to go vegan you had to have super-strong-willpower (funnily enough it doesn't take much willpower for me to not want to eat something that used to be walking around a field), the ability to cook like Gordon Ramsay and be an fountain of knowledge about vegan food. Luckily, none of that turned out to be true. The only thing that mattered was how much we really wanted it, and after a few months we decided that we really did truly want to now revolutionise our diets and therefore our health. If you are struggling with the decision about whether you want to go vegan or not, you need to identify your main reasons for wanting to do so. Perhaps it's because you want to reduce the amount of animal suffering in the world, perhaps it's because you want to reduce your contribution to climate change, maybe it's because you want to lose weight and improve your health. For me and my husband, it was the positive benefits to our health that we most wanted to experience and to drastically reduce our chances of falling victim to any number of horrible diseases later in life (more on this later). We wanted so much to give our bodies the respect that they deserved and only fuel them with nutritious and healthy food. So, whatever your reason is, grasp it tightly with both hands, believe in yourself and your ability to change and adapt and, before you know it, you'll wake up on your one-year-vegan anniversary and you'll wonder what you were worrying about.

There are lots of factors at play that could prevent someone from going vegan, so cut yourself some slack! Just remember that all you need to do is really want to make the change and you will do it. By reading this book you are already taking a big step in the right direction. You, and only you, have the power to make decisions about your life and if being vegan is something that you want to do, then you can do it! The only thing stopping you is you, so it's time to connect to what you really want to do and make the change to make your life better.

So, let's get to it! Each chapter that lies ahead will contain advice, ideas and tips to help make your transition into veganism as smooth as possible.

2. 'NORMAL' FOOD THAT IS ACTUALLY VEGAN

First of all, I want to begin by tackling that big question head on: "What do vegans actually eat?" Now, a lot of people, when asking a vegan this question, don't seem to realise that they probably eat 'vegan' food every day! So, to ease us in to the first part of our journey, I thought it would be nice to identify some of the things that you probably eat already and can still continue eating when vegan. You might be surprised at close you already are to being vegan! So here goes:

- Bread
- Pasta
- Spaghetti
- Rice
- ALL fruits!
- ALL vegetables!
- Potato-based products such as waffles, hash browns and chips
- Baked beans
- Flour
- Some dark chocolate (such as Cadbury Bournville)
- Some biscuits and sweets (such as Skittles)

- Some cereals (such as Shreddies – even the cocoa ones!)
- Some crisps
- Porridge oats

And that is not an exhaustive list by any means! As you can see, there are a lot of things that may already be a part of your daily eating habits that are actually vegan, so you are halfway there already! You can see that I have also included some foods that wouldn't be considered particularly 'healthy' (e.g. sweets and chips!) but this book is about helping you to create your own path through the world of veganism and it's good to know about some of the 'normal' foods that are available.

Of course, though, there will be some exceptions to the list above. For example: some varieties of pasta are made with egg; some types of bread, such as brioche, can be made with egg and some snack items like crisps have milk solids in (weird, right?). So, when you first start your new vegan diet, you will probably need to check ingredients lists carefully until you become more confident in knowing what you can and can't eat.

3. SIMPLE FOOD SWAPS

We are very lucky to live in these modern times because it wouldn't have been as easy to go vegan say ten, twenty or even just five years ago! These days, lots more people are starting to eat vegan diets so there are loads of products, which would traditionally be animal-based, that are now available in alternative, plant-based forms. Most of which are now available in your local supermarket or independent, plant-based retailer (if you're lucky enough to have one nearby!) Let's have a look at some of those now:

- **Milk** – this is one that most animal-eaters will buy weekly, if not daily. There are now lots of simple and tasty swaps for this such as oat, soya, almond or coconut milk.
- **Butter** – a main ingredient in many cakes and a staple for sandwiches. Some of the main butter brands, such as Flora, now produce completely plant-based versions of butter. You can also get olive and sunflower-based spreads.
- **Cheese** – possibly the most popular sandwich ingredient of all time? Many vegan cheeses are coconut-based and come in block, sliced or grated forms.

- **Ham** – maybe the second most popular sandwich ingredient of all time? Ham-style and chicken-style slices can be a nice addition to your lunchtime sandwich.
- **Yoghurt** – a popular 'healthy' snack. Can be found in much healthier soya-based forms in the fridge aisle.
- **Cream** – always nice to have with dessert or maybe in hot drinks. Much like the milk, there are alternative available such as soya and oat-based single or whipped creams.
- **Bacon** – yes, you did read that correctly! There are now companies out there that make vegan 'bacon'.
- **Pasta sauce** – useful to keep in the cupboard for those days you don't want to make your own sauce. Most tomato-based sauces are already vegan but there are now plenty of vegan alternatives available, even 'cheesy' versions!
- **Burgers** – barbeque season? No problem! Whether you prefer chicken-style, hamburger-style or even pulled-pork-style burgers, there is a vegan option out there for you!
- **Sausages** – maker of the big breakfast. Chipolatas, bangers, Lincolnshire, cocktail or Cumberland, your vegan breakfasts or Sunday dinners don't need to be sausage-less.
- **Chicken** – a frequent addition to pasta dishes and stir-fries. Vegan 'chicken' in a shredded form is now widely available.
- **Pizza** – the beloved Friday night treat! Frequent vegan toppings include onion, peppers, jackfruit, sweetcorn and vegan cheese.
- **Mince** – usually used to beef-up (pardon the pun) spaghetti dishes. There are now a few different versions of vegan mince available, all very easy to cook in a jiffy.
- **Egg** – toast's best friend. Why not whip yourself up some plant-based scrambled eggs to start your day

sunny side up?

- **Oils** – such as vegetable or sunflower. These are often used in vegan cake recipes.

4. BUILDING A MEAL

Before we get into the nitty-gritty of how to make delicious vegan meals, I want to first point out the differences between two different types of vegan diet which are: a traditional vegan diet or a whole-foods plant-based (WFPB) diet. Whilst both a WFPB and a vegan diet avoid all animal products (i.e. meat, dairy, eggs and fish), the main difference is that a WFPB diet also avoids things like oils and highly-processed foods. For example, a person following the WFPB diet would mainly stick to eating fruits, vegetables, legumes (beans!) and whole-grains (like whole-wheat bread and pasta) – think of it as food in its most natural form. A vegan would also eat these things but also may occasionally eat things like white bread (which isn't a whole-grain), foods made with white, bleached flour (again, not a whole-grain) and maybe some ready-made vegan foods such as frozen burgers or vegan pre-packaged snacks which have gone through some form of processing to reach their current shape – think about how you can't exactly go and pick a vegan burger from a tree! Safe to say then that a WFPB diet would be considered healthier than a traditional vegan diet but a traditional vegan diet is still MUCH healthier than a non-vegan diet!

You might wonder why I mentioned the WFPB diet. It's because, when people learn that someone is vegan, they typically tend to think that all they eat is raw vegetables and lots of fruit. This is closer to the WFPB strand of the vegan diet and although it is the healthier form of vegan diet, it is not the only way to do it. One of the things that can seem quite off-putting about becoming vegan is the idea that you can only eat super-healthy foods and never eat anything not made from-scratch. Although this is how it may appear if you search social media for vegan recipe ideas, this certainly isn't the case. You can still be vegan and healthier than a meat-eater even if you do occasionally eat pre-prepared vegan foods like vegan sausages or burgers! I certainly found that for the first few months of begin vegan, I would just swap what I used to eat for a vegan-version of it. For example, spaghetti bolognaise with vegan mince or fajitas with vegan 'chicken'-style pieces.

When you first make the switch to veganism, it can seem strange to build a meal which doesn't include a main 'protein' source, as we are all taught that meals should be made up of a main protein, with a side of carbohydrates and vegetables. Think about the meal plate that you probably learnt about in primary school! Just quickly, I want to dispel the myth that vegans don't get any protein – this is absolute nonsense as plants are actually the place where the animals, that you used to eat, get their protein from, so you won't be going without (A.U.M Films and Media 2015). Plants are also full of fibre and antioxidants which are essential for good health and they also don't contain cholesterol which we all know is bad for our bodies. So, when you create your meals, they may appear to be mainly only carbohydrates and vegetables but don't worry, the protein will be in there too! When I first became vegan, I used to keep track of the amount of protein I had because I wanted to be sure that I was getting enough. Safe to say though that I didn't do this for long! I soon realised that I was getting plenty and, like Dr Garth Davis says, I've never met a vegan (or anyone) with a protein deficiency! Also, carbohydrates tend to get a bad name but we can't live without them, they are the building blocks of the energy that our bodies need to function. Don't be concerned if you find yourself eating more rice or potatoes etc than you normally would, it's only the sugary carbs such as in cakes and pastries that it's best not to eat a lot of. So, learn to love carbs because they love you!

Anyway, let's get into building a meal now. Remember we mentioned the food plate (or food pyramid) earlier and how that was split up into categories of protein, carbohydrate and vegetables? I want you to forget about that now and instead, take a look at the lists below.

These foods are the main staples of the vegan diet and you can easily create a delicious meal simply by choosing ingredients from the lists below and combining them to make a meal. These lists aren't exhaustive but they have got enough information for you to make a great start on your journey to veganism.

Grains

(Quick note, with grains it is always best to go for the wholegrain options as these are much healthier for you than the unrefined grain versions because the unrefined versions have had the valuable nutrients, which are naturally in the wholegrains, removed from them. So, swap bleached, white pasta for wholegrain pasta, swap white rice for brown rice and white bread for wholegrain bread).

- Pasta
- Spaghetti
- Bread
- Porridge oats
- Rice
- Quinoa
- Couscous

Vegetables

- Potatoes (white, sweet)
- Peppers
- Spinach
- Tomatoes
- Onions
- Carrots
- Sweetcorn
- Mushroom
- Lettuce
- Broccoli
- Cauliflower

Legumes And Beans

- Kidney beans
- Black beans
- Pinto beans
- Baked beans
- Lentils (red, green, yellow)
- Split peas
- Soy beans
- Chick peas

Fruits

- Peach
- Plum
- Pear
- Apples
- Oranges
- Bananas

- Mango
- Strawberry
- Raspberry
- Blueberry
- Cherry
- Melon
- Avocado

Nuts And Seeds

- Cashew nuts
- Peanuts
- Sunflower seeds
- Flax seeds
- Walnuts
- Almonds
- Pecans
- Pine nuts
- Brazil nuts
- Hazelnuts
- Pumpkin seeds

You might find that the meals you create don't necessarily represent normal or traditional meat-based dishes and this is ok! Sometimes my favourite meals are just a mish-mash of different things that I fancy. Let's use these lists above and come up with a few ideas below of simple meals that could be created with these ingredients.

Potato-Based Meal Ideas

- Baked potato with baked beans (one of the easiest vegan meals!)

- Mashed potato with sweetcorn, peas and roasted carrots *(Top tip! Add a tin of chickpeas into your potatoes when they have about 5 minutes left to go on the stove, then mash these up with the potatoes to add a bit of extra protein and goodness)*
- Boiled potatoes with roasted peppers, mushrooms and cherry tomatoes

Grain-Based Meal Ideas

- Brown rice cooked in vegetable stock with roasted vegetables and gem lettuce leaves
- Wholemeal pasta with basil pesto and roasted broccoli
- Wholemeal spaghetti with kidney beans, chopped tomatoes and onions on top

Vegetable-Based Meal Ideas

- Wholemeal fajita wraps with stir-fried peppers, mushrooms, black beans, and sweetcorn filling
- Roasted peppers, mushrooms, tomatoes, carrots, broccoli with quinoa

(Top tip! It's always best to avoid boiling vegetables as the nutrients all leak out of the vegetables into the water. The closer your vegetables are to raw, the better, I like to roast them for a short time with a bit of black pepper)

Breakfast Ideas

- Porridge with chopped blueberries, raspberries and a sprinkling of sunflower and flax seeds
- Wholemeal bread toast with peanut butter
- Pancakes made with vegan butter and oat milk topped

with bananas and strawberries

So, all you need to do to create your own vegan meal ideas is to choose a starting ingredient from one of the lists above – go with whatever you fancy – and then select some other ingredients to go with it, simple! Try to have a mix of ingredients from across the different types of food, just to remind you, they were: grains, vegetables, legumes/beans, fruits and nuts and seeds. Also, the more colourful you can make your meal – by choosing ingredients of different colours – the better. Different colours mean different vitamins and nutrients so try to have a wide range of colours in your meals.

5. VEGAN SHOPPING LIST

As a vegan, there are certain items that you will find yourself repeatedly buying, so it is a good idea to keep a stock of these things in the cupboards. In this chapter we are going to cover items that will likely be on your weekly shopping list and handy cupboard-fillers.

First of all, let's have a think about herbs and spices. Most vegan recipes that you will come across will include at least one or two different herbs or spices. If you are anything like me, I never used to cook meals from scratch as a meat-eater so I pretty much didn't own any herbs or spices except from salt and pepper. Anything I did make was normally with a pre-made jar of sauce which already had flavouring in. So, when I first came to attempt cooking vegan recipes that I found online, I had to go out and buy a stock of a range of different flavourings as I literally didn't own any! So below I have included a list of what I think are the most common herbs and spices used in recipes that are good to keep handy in your cupboard. These are all referring to the ground versions that you can buy in small jars or pots; fresh versions of some are available but these ground, jarred versions have a long expiration date and are handy to keep in the cupboard.

Herbs And Spices To Keep Stock Of

- Basil
- Cayenne Pepper
- Chinese five-spice
- Chilli powder
- Cinnamon
- Crushed chili
- Coriander
- Cumin
- Garam masala
- Garlic granules
- Garlic powder
- Ginger
- Italian herbs
- Mixed herbs
- Mixed spice
- Nutmeg
- Oregano
- Piri Piri seasoning
- Paprika
- Parsley
- Rosemary
- Thyme
- Turmeric

Of course, there are many more herbs and spices than just these. However, I have found that these seem to be the main ones that vegan recipes call for, so these are the ones that I always keep a stock of. Sometimes if I discover a new recipe which requires seasonings that I don't have, I will just add them to my shopping list and get them the next time I go shopping.

Things To Keep In The Cupboard

Below I have listed a range of ingredients which are often used in vegan recipes and you will find yourselves using frequently so it's a good idea to keep these in stock. As a vegan friend of my husband's once said when we told him we had gone vegan and how we'd had to buy all of these strange new foods: you'll find that you'll have tins of chickpeas coming out of your ears! Which is funny because it's so true!

- Chickpeas
- Chopped tomatoes
- Baked beans
- Kidney beans
- Black beans
- Vegetable stock cubes
- Nutritional yeast flakes (sounds weird I know but good for making 'cheese' sauces)
- Sunflower oil
- Vegetable oil
- Olive oil
- Wholewheat pasta
- Wholewheat spaghetti
- Brown rice
- Quinoa
- A range of nuts and seeds
- Pearl barley
- Green lentils
- Red lentils
- Porridge oats

Fresh Ingredients To Have On Your Weekly Shopping List

Here is a list of foods that I find that I am buying on a weekly basis as they are fresh and usually all gone within a week.

- Spinach
- Kale
- Broccoli
- Gem lettuce
- Peppers
- Cauliflower
- Apples
- Oranges
- Bananas
- Frozen sweetcorn
- Frozen peas
- White baking potatoes
- Sweet potatoes
- Salad
- Plant-based butter
- Oat milk
- Wholegrain bread
- Wholegrain wraps
- Toast topping such as jam or Marmite (yep, Marmite is vegan all you Marmite lovers out there!)

Of course, you don't have to buy these exact items and I'm sure that there are foods that I've not mentioned which you will want to buy too. These are just a handy suggestion of the sort of things you might find yourself buying.

One of the other things which can take some getting used to when you first start shopping as a vegan is label-reading. There will be some products which you will need to check the labels of the make sure that they don't have any animal products in. Once you start looking at labels, you will be surprised how many items have animal products in! Even things like crisps, pesto and biscuits – not exactly meaty items! – often have some form of animal product in. Here is a handy list of things that you will want to be looking out for when you do your shopping and some of the different ways that they can be listed on ingredients labels:

- Milk: milk solids/ whey/ lactose/ casein/ khoya/ malai/ cultured dextrose
- Butter: buttermilk/ ghee/ curds/ lard
- Egg: albumen
- Honey/ royal jelly
- Fish: fish sauce/ cod liver oil/ anchovy/ isinglass/ aspic/ shellfish
- Other animal bits and pieces (quite literally): gelatine/ rennet/ carmine/ castoreum/ shellac/ lanolin/ beeswax

Again, this is not an exhaustive list. It is up to you how in-depth you would like to be when checking ingredients lists. For example, some products might say 'may contain milk' and this tends to just mean that the item was produced in a factory which also handles milk products. Some vegans may avoid these products but others don't. Personally, I will still eat these products (as long as everything else included is vegan!) as I feel that the item hasn't been produced using milk and it's unlikely that they have actually come into contact with any milk – this warning is usually for people who have allergies. Luckily, most products nowadays have allergens labelled in bold on their ingredients list and usually in a clear and simple form (milk, eggs, butter etc). There are also a lot of products now which are actually labelled as being vegan too, which makes life much easier for us! Also, most places now have dedicated 'free-from' or 'plant-based' sections where you will find specific vegan products, which is always handy.

Top tip! When shopping, it is still worth checking the label of products that haven't been specifically labelled as vegan. As you will sometimes discover things that are actually vegan when you read the ingredients list, but because they're not labelled as being vegan, they can often be a lot cheaper! I was delighted recently when I found a pack of dark-chocolate biscuits in my local super-market that was actually vegan although it didn't explicitly say so, and because they weren't labelled as 'vegan biscuits', they didn't cost the Earth! Although this isn't to say that vegan-specific products are always expensive, I have just personally found that they seem to cost a bit more than non-vegan products. For example, the packet of dark-chocolate biscuits that I mentioned earlier were 60p for a 500g pack, whereas if I bought a packet of dark-chocolate biscuits that were marketed as being vegan-friendly, this would have cost me closer to £2 for the pack.

When I first became vegan, I found shopping took me a lot longer than usual because I was getting used to reading labels and try-ing to figure out what I could actually buy and I used to find it quite stressful. Which is why I have included this chapter because I think I would have found it a lot easier if someone had given me some ideas about what I should buy – so I hope this has helped you!

Eating Out

Since we are on the subject of what foods we can and can't buy to eat, I thought it would be worth making a note on the sub-ject of dining-out as a vegan. Luckily, most places nowadays have got specific vegan options on their menus as veganism and plant-based diets become more popular, which makes life a lot easier. Of course, if it is a steakhouse that you're hoping to go to though, I'm not sure how many vegan options they would have! One old-faithful friend of vegans eating-out is the humble portion of chips! Oh potatoes, how we worship thee... If you do fancy yourself a portion of chips though, it can be worth asking what these are cooked in, as some places fry their chips in beef dripping, as opposed to vegetable oil, or some places cook them in the same fryers as meat products. Again, this is one of those occasions where personal preference comes into play, as some folks might not mind this particularly but others will. I personally don't eat chips that have been cooked in beef-dripping or with other animal products but it's up to you. Back to the main point though, most restaurants and cafes now provide vegan options but it is always worth checking-out their menus online before you visit, so that you are prepared. If you can't see anything listed on their website, most places are happy for you to give them a call and ask if they do provide any vegan options, and even if they don't have any specific items, a lot of places are happy to make a dish specially as long as you book ahead. So, it's worth doing your research and finding out what's on the menu before you head out to a restaurant.

6. MY FOOD DIARY
FOR ONE WEEK

N ow that we have discussed different foods that you can eat and what you should stock your cupboards with, I thought it would be useful to see how this actually looks in practice by taking a normal week of my life and recording what I ate. Remember, I don't pretend to be the healthiest vegan on the planet and I have written this book for normal people like you and me, so don't be surprised when you see vegan ice-cream on the list!

Note: everything on the list below is a vegan version of a product, even if I haven't specifically labelled it as being so (for example, 'cheese' would actually be vegan cheese).

Monday

Breakfast: Marmite on toast using wholemeal bread and sunflower spread

Lunch: Wholemeal wrap with lettuce, tomatoes and cheese

Dinner: Spaghetti puttanesca with chopped tomatoes, chickpeas and kale

Tuesday

Breakfast: Strawberry jam on toast using wholemeal bread and sunflower spread

Lunch: Cold pasta with chopped tomatoes, sweetcorn

Dinner: Homemade-pizza made with pre-rolled pizza dough, with tomatoes, mushrooms and olives

Wednesday

Breakfast: Porridge with oat milk

Lunch: Jacket potato with baked beans

Dinner: Lentil chilli with brown rice

Thursday

Breakfast: Cocoa spread on toast with wholemeal bread

Lunch: Oven-baked baguette with tomatoes and cheese

Dinner: Chinese-style fried rice with mushrooms and peas

Friday

Breakfast: Smoothie made with bananas, oranges, apples, oat milk, nuts and seeds

Lunch: Jacket potato with houmous and pesto

Dinner: Whole wheat spaghetti mixed with pesto and roasted mushrooms and peppers

Saturday

Breakfast: Bowl of cocoa shreddies with oat milk

Lunch: Quinoa with gem lettuce, cherry tomatoes and cucumber

Dinner: Potato and cauliflower curry with brown rice

Sunday

Breakfast: Crumpets with marmite and sunflower spread

Lunch: Pancakes made with oat milk with fruit, berries and some cocoa spread for good measure!

Dinner: Mashed potatoes with peas and sausages. Chocolate cake with vanilla ice cream for dessert in the evening.

As you can see, I am certainly no chef and even though I am vegan, I certainly didn't starve or become reduced to just eating beans because I couldn't find anything else to eat! It really is possible to still eat lots of delicious foods when you are vegan. In fact, I would definitely say that I discovered far more foods and began expanding my taste buds when I became vegan. I rarely would have ventured down the vegetable aisle in my meat-eating days but now I'm always there!

In my diary, I didn't note any snacks that I ate because I found that, I didn't really snack at all between meals. To be honest, this did actually surprise me a bit because, when I was a meat-eater, I would snack constantly and on all of the wrong things. This is most likely because plant-based food has far more nutrients, minerals, carbs and fibre that our bodies need to function, so each meal carries me easily to the next one without getting cravings in the gap. Whereas, animal-based products are particularly lacking in everything that we need, so they don't really fill us up properly and they can't sustain our bodies for very long, hence wanting to snack more frequently. The only time I did snack was having a couple of biscuits with a cup of tea in the evening after dinner, usually Oreos (yes, at the time of writing this, the original Oreos are vegan - hallelujah!)

7. ACTUALLY
SIMPLE RECIPES

One of my biggest issues with vegan recipes that you find in recipe books and on the internet, is that they are always so damn complicated! The worst part is though, is that they are often labelled as 'simple', 'beginner' or 'easy' recipes when they clearly are not! As I mentioned earlier, I was no good at cooking when I was a meat-eater and I relied heavily on frozen food and jarred sauces. So when I decided to become vegan, it really was a huge shock to the system as I realised that, for the first time in my life, I was going to have to learn how to cook if I wanted to experience all the great benefits of delicious, healthy vegan food and not just rely on frozen vegan-options like I was used to with frozen animal-products. It did take me a few months to get used to actually cooking things that were fresh and following recipes but I got there in the end and although I am by no means an amazing cook now, I am definitely one-hundred times better than I was before I was vegan!

Getting back to recipes, I used to spend hours upon hours trawling the internet to find vegan recipes that I wanted to use but I came across several issues when doing this:

a) They always seemed to contain hundreds of ingredients!
b) Of these ingredients, there were always so many that I had never heard of before, let alone have experience of cooking with!
c) The method always seemed SOOOO complicated! Like having to soak things all night before summoning up the god of vegan cooking by doing a magical rain dance. Like seriously, way too complicated for someone with the cooking skills of an 8-year-old.

So, in this chapter, you will find some meal-ideas that I have put together. I wouldn't exactly call them 'recipes' because they are not quite in that format. To be honest, I put them together in a style that I would have found accessible and understandable when I first became vegan so these are designed to be useful for you lovely people who are new to the world of veganism and vegan cooking. If vegan cooking was made to seem easier, I bet more people would become vegan and therefore experience the amazing health benefits of veganism – now wouldn't that be great?!

Lunch Recipes

Ok so let's start with a few ideas about different lunches that you can make to have either at home or to take with you to work.

Pesto pasta

This is one that my husband loves and can be eaten hot straight away or is still delicious cold later if you want to have it for lunch. If you do want to have this for lunch and are preparing it the evening before, let it cool down after cooking and then pop it in a sealed lunch box in the fridge overnight. I would recommend preparing it the night before, rather than in the morning, unless you know you'll have time to let it cool down before you head off to work because you don't want it to sweat in the lunch box.

All you need is: (Love! Well, that and these few ingredients…)

- Spaghetti (whole-wheat is healthier but it's up to you) – the amount you have is up to you but I usually find that a quarter of a packet does one person plenty (around 100g/125g or so)
- A jar of pesto (be sure to get this from the 'free-from' aisle or make sure it is a vegan version). Any flavour of pesto is fine, whichever you prefer! I like basil or sundried tomato.
- A selection of vegetables that you can roast. I like to have mushrooms, peppers and broccoli.

Now what?

- Cook the spaghetti. A little tip: if you are making this to take for lunch then it is easier to break up the spaghetti into small pieces first so that it is easier to eat with a fork or spoon out of a lunchbox later. Also, I find if you boil the water first, either in the kettle or on the hob, then add the spaghetti, it's far less likely to go soggy then if you start with cold water. If you like watching Hell's Kitchen then you'll know that the spaghetti should only take 7 minutes! (Or is it 8? Gordon please forgive me if you're reading this!) And don't forget to put some salt in the water too to give the spaghetti a bit of flavour (thanks Gordon!) Keep stirring the spaghetti every minute or so when it's cooking so it doesn't stick together. When you get to around 7 minutes, take a piece out to test every minute or so until you think it is done. It shouldn't be crunchy but you don't want it to be soggy either.
- Before you put your spaghetti on, preheat the oven to about 180°C for a fan oven, ready for your vegetables. Whilst your spaghetti is cooking, wash and prepare your

vegetables. I usually cut the mushrooms into quarters; cut the peppers in half and then slice up each half into chunks and then cut off a few stalks of broccoli. When you've done this, grab yourself a baking tray (you can also line it with foil first) and lightly coat it with a squirt or two of a spray oil (like sunflower oil spray or olive oil spray) before then spreading out your vegetables on the tray. Top tip: I like to sprinkle a little bit of sea salt and cracked black pepper onto the tray before I add the vegetables and then a little bit more pepper over the top of the vegetables as a little bit of extra seasoning. Now pop the tray in the oven and lightly roast them. They should be done at about the same time at the spaghetti, normally only 5 minutes or so as you just want to give them a light roasting so they keep most of their crunchiness. However, remember that you don't have to roast your vegetables at all and you can have them raw! Pepper and broccoli have a nice crunch and still taste delicious raw.

-    When your spaghetti is done, drain it and leave it in the saucepan. Now add in about a heaped teaspoon of the pesto and mix this in. Give it a little taste-test, you might find that you prefer a bit more pesto so add in little bits more and keep tasting until you're happy. Now spoon this out onto your plate. Grab the vegetables out of the oven and add these on top of the spaghetti – it doesn't have to be a masterpiece so don't worry about how you do this! Et voila! Lunch is served.

Pizza baguette

I have to admit – this is one of my favourite lunches to make when I am working from home as it is quick and easy but still tasty!

All you need is:

-      A baguette – cut a good length off and slice this in half sideways so that you have two pieces
-      Tomato passata – usually found near the beans or chopped tomatoes in the supermarket aisle, it can come in bottles, cartons or cans (I prefer the bottled version as I never normally use a whole one at once so it can be more easily stored and resealed to be kept in the fridge until next time you need it).
-      Toppings – not too many though as you don't want to make the baguette soggy. I usually have sliced tomatoes and a few sliced black olives
-      Vegan cheese
-      Any flavouring you might like. Perhaps a sprinkling of basil for a classic taste or maybe some paprika to spice it up a bit?

Now what?

-      Take your pre-sliced baguette and pop it on a baking tray (or pizza trays work well for this too). Pre-heat the oven to about 180/200°C for a fan oven.
-      Dollop about two tablespoons of passata onto the baguette and spread around evenly but not too thick as you don't want it to be soggy. I usually find this easier to do with the back of a tablespoon rather than a knife.
-      Depending on how you like your cheese, you can add it now or later. If I'm using sliced cheese, I like to lay it on top of the passata, with a couple of slices to cover the whole baguette.
-      Now add your toppings. I slice the tomatoes thinly and lay these on top of the baguette then sprinkle some sliced black olives on top of these.
-      Add your seasoning. Maybe you add a sprinkling of sea salt and black pepper too if you like, or other flavourings like your basil or paprika. If you're using basil, pour a little bit into the palm of your hand first and then use the other hand

to pinch and sprinkle it on – I find it much easier to control this way rather than sprinkling straight out of the pot and putting too much on!

- You might also choose to add your cheese now. If I'm using grated cheese, I usually like to add it at the end, sprinkled on top of everything else. Or, if you really want to spice things up about, why not have sliced cheese on the bottom and some grated on the top?
- Now pop the baking tray in the oven. These usually take between 5-10 minutes so I would recommend keeping a close eye on them so that you can see the bread cooking and take it out when it's to your desired crunchiness!

Quinoa salad

Now I'm hoping that you haven't seen the word 'quinoa' (pronounced keen-wah) and broken into a cold sweat. This is one of those foods which I used to think was only eaten by people who were amazing chefs, yoga masters or something else with amazing Instagram photos. But never fear, friends! You too can eat the fabled quinoa and it's not as strange or scary as you think.

All you need is:
- About half a cup of quinoa
- Gem lettuce
- Cherry tomatoes
- Cucumber
- Any other delicious fruit or veg you would like to add!
- Vegetable stock cubes (x2)

Now what?

- First of all, let's get that quinoa cooking. Pour your quinoa into a saucepan and add boiling water from the kettle. Or boil the water so it's bubbling away in the pan first and then add the quinoa – your choice! Now crumble in the stock cubes – how many you use here is your choice, I prefer using two cubes but you might find that you would prefer one in the future. Or you might not want to use the stock cubes at all, I just find that it gives the quinoa a nice flavour. Make sure to give this all a stir every couple of minutes.

- Whilst the quinoa is on, wash your gem lettuce and then dry and chop up into small pieces. OR you can leave the leaves whole and use them to scoop up the quinoa with!

- Now chop your cherry tomatoes in half and slice up your cucumber.

- After about 10 minutes or so, the quinoa will be done. You will be able to tell if it is done because the little kernels will look like they have popped open. If not, then leave it slightly longer. Now to drain the quinoa; this can be a bit tricky as the kernels are so tiny, so I always use a sieve to do this.

- You can serve this in a variety of ways. I like to use a large plate or bowl and arrange everything around the plate into separate sections. But you can do this however you want to; you may like the quinoa on the bottom of the plate first with all of the lovely fruit and veg scattered on top. Or I'm sure there must be a very Instagram-worthy way of arranging this meal if that's what you're into!

Dinner Recipes

Ok so hopefully you found those lunch recipes useful. Now let's move on to dinner recipes. These are all designed for 2 people so either half the portions for just one person or save the leftovers for the following day!

Chinese-style rice

This recipe was born when I had a hankering for some Chinese-style fried-rice but the only Chinese restaurant near me didn't have any vegan options for their rice. So, I decided to try and make my own and it actually turned out to be rather tasty! The combination of the sesame oil to cook in and the 5-spice seasoning gave it that Chinese-style flavour and the mushrooms and peas reminded me of the mushroom-fried rice I used to have from the takeaway. This is also very nice to have cold for lunch the following day – bonus!

All you need is:

-     1 cup of rice (I used brown)
-     Closed cup mushrooms (maybe about 5, or more if you really love mushrooms!)
-     Garden peas (I use frozen and about ¾ of a cup full)
-     Sesame oil
-     Salt
-     Pepper
-     Chinese 5-spice seasoning

Now what?

Now I'm sure there might be a 'proper' or better way of doing this but this is the way I did it!

-     Boil the rice first. This normally takes a while to cook, maybe about 30-40 minutes.
-     Whilst this is cooking, wash the mushrooms and chop them into quarters.
-     When the rice is done, drain it and then leave it in the

saucepan.
- In a wok or stir-fry pan, add a teaspoon or two worth of the sesame oil and turn up the heat to about medium.
- Now add the peas and stir regularly for about three minutes.
- Now add the mushrooms and again, stir for a couple of minutes.
- Add a sprinkling of the 5-spice seasoning now and stir
- Next, add the rice. Before you mix it all in, sprinkle more of the 5-spice seasoning on top with some salt and pepper too. Then, get mixing! Stir everything together and keep stirring to get a nice even coverage of the seasoning. Cook for a few more minutes, constantly stirring. Give it a taste and add more seasoning if you need to.

Fajitas

I LOVE fajitas! They are super quick and easy to make and delicious too. I like to make this in a big wok and put this on the table afterwards with a big spoon so people can serve it straight from the wok into their wraps. The great thing about this recipe is that you can change the amount of vegetables to suit you – so add more sweetcorn if you love sweetcorn! And you can add in or leave out vegetables as you wish, you can mix and match from your favourite vegetables.

All you need is:

- Tortilla wraps (wholemeal is healthiest)
- Olive oil
- A tin of black beans

- 2 bell peppers (I like to use different colours!)
- Closed cup mushrooms
- Frozen sweetcorn
- 1 red onion
- Broccoli
- Optional: Kale/spinach. Chopped tomatoes if you want a bit more juiciness.
- Seasoning: you can either choose your own like paprika or you can often purchase fajita-seasoning pre-made which is normally found in the seasoning aisle

Now what?

- Pour a tablespoon or so worth of olive oil into the wok and turn on the heat to a medium heat.
- Peel and chop the onion
- Put the onion into the wok along with about half a cup full of sweetcorn and stir
- Drain the beans and add these in after a couple of minutes and stir
- Add chopped tomatoes now if using them
- Chop up the peppers and remove the seeds. Add these in and stir
- Chop up the broccoli, add in and stir
- Slice up the mushrooms and add these in and stir
- You don't want to cook for too much longer after adding the mushrooms in because they will release all of their water and reduce too much – maybe 2 minutes.
- If you want to add anything extra like kale or spinach then add these at the end as they reduce quickly and you want them to keep a bit of crunchiness.
- Add a good sprinkling of your seasoning and stir, sprinkle a bit more and stir again to coat all of the ingredients nicely (use more or less depending on your preference)
- Turn the heat off and voila! Your filling is now ready.

- You can put the wok straight onto a placemat on the table and have wraps ready on plates so you can dish straight up into the wraps.
- Other nice things to add at this point could include salsa, cheese or some crunchy gem lettuce leaves!

Vegetable lasagne

This is a bit of a longer one to prepare but is definitely worth it because it's so tasty and satisfying! This can be cut into 6 portions and put with some salad or potato wedges as a side, or if you're hungry makes a very filling dinner for two people (and maybe even some left over!). This recipe includes vegan cheese sauce which would take the place of the usual white lasagne sauce. This can be left out if preferred.

All you need is:

- Lasagne sheets (check to make sure they don't have egg in them)
- 2 tins kidney beans
- About 6 medium-sized mushrooms
- 1 tin chopped tomatoes (or 2 if you like it more tomatoey – that's now a word!)
- 2 bell peppers (seeds removed and diced)
- 1 red onion
- 3 medium cloves of garlic
- 2 or 3 good-sized handfuls of kale or spinach (I prefer kale in this dish)
- Any other veg you fancy (I also like to add broccoli)
- 1 tsp basil
- 1 tsp oregano
- 2 tsp paprika

For the cheese sauce
- 1 tablespoon butter
- 2 tablespoons plain flour

- 250-300ml oat or soya milk
- Nutritional yeast flakes (sounds weird I know but can be found in most supermarkets, this gives the sauce its cheesy flavour)
- 1 tsp of paprika (add more if you want to spice the sauce up a little)

Now what?

Start by preparing the lasagne filling.

- Put the onion and garlic in a large pan with some olive oil over a medium heat (I like to use a wok for pretty much all cooking like this!)
- Now add the peppers (and broccoli if using) and stir
- Sprinkle on the basil, oregano and paprika
- Add the kidney beans and stir for 1-2 minutes
- Add chopped tomatoes and stir. Add salt and pepper if desired.
- Put in the kale a few bits at a time to let them wilt down as you stir them in
- Chop and add the mushrooms. Give it a stir.
- You can now turn the heat off on this and set it to one side for a few minutes

Now prepare the cheese sauce

- Put a large, heaped tablespoon scoop of butter into a sauce-pan and turn the heat on low until it melts
- Turn the heat off and add a flat tablespoon of plain flour and stir it together – it's easier to use a whisk for this. Keep adding flour a little bit at a time until the butter and flour have combined nicely so it is now not running and a gloopy, almost solid texture. This can be a bit hard to tell, if you add slightly too much flour then the mixture will combine pretty much into a ball of what looks like dough, but this is

ok as we can just add more milk to counteract this.

- Now pour in 250ml of your plant-based milk and put the heat back on low-medium. Keep constantly stirring with your whisk to combine together. You can always add more milk if you think you added too much flour originally or if the mixture thickens too quickly.
- When the mixture has thickened so it is of a custard-type thickness, turn the heat off.
- Now add in two heaped tablespoons of the yeast flakes and stir. You can also add paprika, salt and pepper here if you would like. I usually add about a teaspoon of paprika.

Now it's time to assemble the lasagne!

- Scoop half of the filling from the wok into a large, rectangular glass baking dish.
- Now pour about half of the cheese sauce on top of this, using the back of a tablespoon to spread it around to get a good coverage
- Now lay your lasagne sheets on top of this. I usually use about 3 laying side-by-side.
- Repeat the process: add the rest of the filling, then the rest of the cheese sauce and add more lasagne sheets on top.
- To finish off, I like to sprinkle some grated cheese over the top and a little bit of sea salt.
- Cover the dish with silver foil and pop in the oven at 180 degrees for about 15 minutes. This should be enough time for the pasta to cook through. After the first 15 minutes, you can remove the foil if you want the top layer of pasta sheets to crisp up a little. Just keep checking it every couple of minutes so that it doesn't burn.
- And there we go! A delicious vegan lasagne to satisfy your stomach.

Cheese sauce

The cheese sauce recipe I mentioned above as part of the lasagne recipe can be used for all sorts of different things! I love to also make some to add into fajitas, or even to layer on top of tortilla chips which I then bake in the oven to turn into nachos! You can even cook up some macaroni pasta and then mix it in with this sauce to make macaroni cheese or add it to another pasta dish. This is a great little recipe to keep handy and once you've made it a couple of times, you'll start to get a feel for how thick you like your sauce and can adjust the amount of flour and milk accordingly (less flour/more milk = thinner sauce).

Lentil chilli

This chilli is perfect for a chilly autumn evening (see what I did there?). It can be served on top of rice or a jacket potato. This is another one where you can mix and match with your favourite veggies, adding in extras if you want to. It usually serves 2 people.

All you need is:
- ½ cup of rice or one medium-large baking potato
- 150g red or green dried lentils (or 75g of each!)
- 1 bell pepper (you choose the colour)
- 1 tin kidney beans
- 1 tin chopped tomatoes
- 1 tsp chilli powder
- 1 tsp cumin
- 1 tsp paprika
- 1 red onion
- 2 cloves garlic
- 2 tbsp tomato puree
- Olive oil (could also use sunflower oil)

Now what?

If you are having the jacket potato with this chilli then you will want to get this cooking before you begin. I usually wrap mine in foil and cook it for about 2 hours in a fan oven at about 180 degrees – I like it crispy! However, if you like to microwave yours or cook it for a shorter time, just start to cook it whenever is best to match up with when you are ready to serve your chilli.

- Put your rice on to boil for about 30-40 minutes (if you are having rice instead of a potato)
- Whilst your rice is boiling, dice your onion and add it to your wok with about a teaspoon of olive oil on a medium heat, stirring frequently.
- Add the garlic – you can either finely chop this or use a garlic press (which I find far less fiddly than chopping!)
- Now dice your pepper, making sure to remove the seeds and add this to the pan. Note: If you notice the ingredients starting to stick to the pan at any point then you may need to reduce the heat or add a bit more oil.
- Now add the chilli powder, cumin and paprika and stir a few times before adding the chopped tomatoes and tomato puree.
- Next add your lentils to the wok
- Now add about 1 cup of water – make sure there is a good coverage so the lentils are floating around, add more if not; the lentils will soak up most of it.
- Now let this simmer for about 10 minutes, keep stirring regularly and add more water if it is getting dried out at any point.
- Now drain and add the kidney beans. This is also a good point at which to add any chopped kale or spinach if you would like to – I put these in almost everything! Stir and simmer for another 3-5 minutes.
- Hopefully your rice or potato will be about ready if you started it early enough. Prepare and plate-up your rice or potato however you want to.

- Then you can use a ladle or serving spoon to serve your chilli out onto your potato or rice. Delicious!

More Meal Ideas

Ok so as you can probably tell from the 'recipes' above, I am not exactly a chef! I often just see what I fancy and throw meals together based on that, using the lists of ingredients that I mentioned in a previous chapter. So, what I'm going to do below is list some more meal ideas to hopefully give you a bit of inspiration! Again, everything I note below is a vegan version of that product, so if it says 'cheese' it means a vegan cheese!

Breakfast ideas

- Toast! With a huge variety of toppings: butter, jam, marmite, peanut butter
- Porridge: Can be made with soya, almond, oat or other plant-based milks. You can also add things like fruit and berries for delicious toppings
- Sausage sandwich – a classic!
- Vegan fry-up: could include sausage, beans, hash browns, mushrooms, tomatoes, toast
- Smoothie: use plant-milk based and can include a variety of ingredients. Such as: banana, strawberries, apples, oranges, raspberries, blueberries, mango. You can also add things like vanilla essence or cocoa powder to give it a bit of a different flavour. If using a blender, you can also include nuts and seeds like flax seeds and chia seeds or even porridge oats which gives you a great boost of energy for the morning.

Packed-lunch ides – great for children too!

- Sandwiches: can have any combination of a variety of fill-

ings! E.g. cheese, 'ham' slices, mayo, pickle, tomato, roasted
peppers, cucumber, salad
-       Salads: you can usually find bags of different types of
prepared salads nowadays in shops which make this lunch a
nice and easy one to prepare! Add your choice of extras to
your salad: tomatoes, cucumber, diced peppers, sunflower
seeds etc
-       Fruit: a nice and easy lunchbox filler. Things like apples,
bananas, pears, oranges, grapes all fit nicely into a lunchbox
-       Vegetables: carrot sticks, cucumber sticks, sliced bell peppers, broccoli florets – all are refreshingly tasty raw
-       Pasta: can prepare the night before and mixed with a variety of sauces. You can easily buy jarred sauces if preferred
or just mix with things like chopped tomatoes, passata or
pesto and add any extra ingredients to mix it up a bit
-       Rice: again, like the pasta, this can be prepared the night
before. Add a couple of vegetable stock cubes when cooking
to add some extra flavour.

Dinner ideas

-       Jacket potatoes: the humble potato, you truly are a gift to
all vegans. Spruce up your spud with any toppings you like!
Here are just a few you could choose or mix and match from:
baked beans, chopped tomatoes, kidney beans, kale, spinach, chopped gem lettuce, pesto, salsa, guacamole, hummus.
My favourite toppings are either baked beans or red pesto
and hummus – which may sound like a bit of a strange combination but works very well!
-       Homemade pizza with homemade potato wedges: All
you need to do to make the wedges is chop up a potato into
wedge-shapes and bake in the oven with a little bit of oil
drizzled on them. You can also make your own pizza dough
or buy prepared pizza mixes which you just add water too,
or if you really want to save time then you can buy prepared
pre-rolled dough – so all you need to do is add your toppings!

I use tomato passata for the base sauce and then you can add your favourite toppings! I like sliced salad tomatoes, sliced mushrooms and black olives with a sprinkling of basil.

- Pasta bake: one of my tummy-cuddling favourites! Pasta is another amazing food that be made in so many different ways with so many different ingredients. I like to cook some pasta and then mix it up with either a tin of chopped tomatoes or the cheese sauce I mentioned earlier. Then add a load of my favourite vegetables like chopped bell peppers, sweetcorn, peas, spinach, mix it all together and then pop into a big glass baking dish to put in the oven.

8. VEGANISM FOR WEIGHT-LOSS

I wanted to add this and the next little chapters in because these are both things that have affected me in my personal journey of becoming a vegan.

The reason I became vegan in the first place was because of the many, many health benefits and because I wanted to do everything I could to prevent myself from getting any horrible diseases like heart disease, cancer and diabetes etc later in life and I felt like I needed a change from my previous takeaway-loving self. I mean, I would eat a takeaway or something from a fast-food place and would literally feel like I had, what I described as, 'dirty veins' and straight away afterwards I would feel sluggish and like I could feel like fat and grease pumping around my body. I'm sure lots of people have experienced what's called the 'meat sweats' – when you eat an animal product, your body actually experiences an inflammatory response within just a few hours of you eating that product (Greger 2012).

However, the benefits that I started to experience from becoming vegan started to affect other areas of my life too. I lost a whole stone in weight, just within a few months, and this wasn't because I was actively trying to lose it. I had just replaced all of the bad food in my life with much better, healthier food. And the best thing about it was that I literally ate what I wanted, whenever I wanted! Previously in my life, I had tried to go on several diets and had tried all sorts of calorie-counting, low-fat, supposedly-healthy options and even though I would usually lose a little bit of weight, it would ALWAYS come back on again within the following weeks and months and I would often end up being heavier than what I started at. I can honestly say this since I started being vegan, I haven't counted calories or tried to diet once because I haven't felt like I needed to. The only thing that I have done is kept to a mainly whole-food, plant-based diet. Because, like I mentioned earlier on in the book, it is possible to be a vegan that isn't quite as healthy as a WFPB vegan. Especially if you just rely on pre-packaged, frozen vegan food, vegan fast-food or takeaways and chips! In fact, there are many studies that have shown that a WFPB diet is the best diet you can have if you want to lose weight, compared to other calorie-counting and restrictive diets (Greger 2020). So, although this isn't one of my personal reasons for turning vegan, it is certainly a great benefit and side-effect of becoming vegan! So if you are hoping to lose weight, then the more you stick to the WFPB type of veganism, the more likely you are to lose weight in a healthy way because your body will be getting the nutrients it needs and none of the rubbish that used to make it store so much fat (when was the last time you saw fat on a vegetable or piece of fruit?).

9. VEGANISM FOR ATHLETES / THE PROTEIN PROBLEM

What I do mean by athlete? When I use this term, I'm not just referring to professional sports-people. I am talking about anyone who likes to exercise regularly or who plays or competes in sports regularly. For example, my husband and I personally do a lot of cycling and compete in short-distance events such as 10 or 25-mile time-trials and sprint-triathlons.

So, if you are an athlete and are thinking about becoming vegan and you are worried about not getting enough protein, let me stop you right there. This isn't something that you need to worry about if you are planning to actually eat some plants as part of your vegan diet – sound ridiculous? I know. At this point, I would like to recommend that you read Dr Garth Davis' book *Proteinaholic*. He is absolutely an expert in this area and, if getting enough protein is something that you are concerned about, I found his book very useful in dispelling these worries.

In his book, Dr Davis talks about how the protein myth has taken a hold of our society and how everyone believes that needing a source of protein is the main reason that we need to eat meat. Dr Davis details clearly and precisely why this is not the case and how, actually, we CAN get protein from plants and also how animal protein is harmful to our bodies. Plants actually create the protein that animals then eat, so by cutting out the animal-products you will just be getting protein from its natural source! In fact, the animal protein *casein* which is found in dairy products, has actually been shown to stimulate cancer-cell growth (Campbell and Campbell 2018).

I have been asked before if I count my protein and keep track of how much protein I'm consuming. When I first became vegan, I did do this for a few weeks and kept a diary record of how many grams of protein I ate per day. However, I soon stopped this when I realised that, by eating a mainly whole-foods, plant-based (WFPB) diet, I was getting all of the protein that I needed and was actually getting protein that was far better for my body than the animal protein that I used to consume. In fact, funnily enough, studies have found that the average meat-eater tends to consume more protein than their bodies actually need and this excess animal protein is just turned into a waste or stored as fat (McMacken 2016).

Now, I'm not a doctor and I can't go into elaborate medical detail about exactly how protein functions within the body and how this affects sports-people but what I can talk about is my own experiences. As I mentioned above, me and my husband are both keen cyclists and like to compete in cycling and triathlon events. This means that we train usually at least 3 times per week, mainly cycling with some running too. When we first became vegan, we did so because we wanted to avoid all of the major health problems that are linked to the eating of animal products, so we weren't sure how it was going to affect our sporting performance.

And, boy, were we surprised! After about a month or so of becoming vegan, we started to notice a big change in our energy levels. You know that sluggish feeling you get after eating a big meal full of animal products? We never experienced that anymore because eating plants doesn't make you feel like that – I like to think about how it's because I'm not consuming all of the fat and cholesterol which loves to clog up our arteries... yuck. So, in general, our energy levels were much higher which meant that we had more energy for training.

The biggest thing that we noticed was how different our bodies felt *after* training or an event like a race. Before we were vegan, we would often ache after training sessions (even after stretching and 'protein-shakes') and this would usually last at least the rest of the day and normally the following day too, we would feel stiff and sore. Particularly if we had raced a time-trial or triathlon, we would usually still feel achy for at least a couple or few days afterwards. After being vegan for about a month, all of that changed. We were absolutely amazed to find that our recovery time had decreased dramatically. In fact, after a few months, the recovery period had pretty much disappeared. Right now, after being vegan for almost two years, I can safely say that I feel like I've pretty much recovered by the time I've had a shower after a training session and, even after a race, I normally feel fine once I've eaten and had a little stretch. Then I'm ready to go again! This really has had a huge impact on our training because before, we were never physically able to train two days in a row, let alone 3 or 4 days in a row which we do sometimes do now. We always used to need at least one empty day in between training days so that we could recover fully – not anymore! Which means that we can now train for longer and more frequently, which is obviously beneficial if you are training for specific events.

As well as feeling much better within ourselves and being able to get the most out of our training, if you are anything like me (a little competitive...) then you'll know that the proof is in the pudding. We became vegan in December 2018, which was during the 'winter training' season so it wasn't until the next season began in Spring 2020 that we would see any results. During that season, my husband and I both achieved personal-best times in our 10 and 25-mile cycling time trials and we both won our age group prizes at least once in sprint triathlons. For the number-lovers, in my 10-mile cycling time trial, I finally managed to get under 30 minutes and managed to get a PB of 27:46 – which is a huge improvement!

So, the moral of this chapter is that I absolutely swear by my vegan diet when it comes to my athletic performance. Nowadays I do my best to mainly keep to a WFPB diet but when I first went vegan, I did rely on a lot of frozen stuff and pre-prepared vegan food, and even then, it still made a difference to my performance when compared to my animal-eating days. But for optimal performance, I would recommend staying as close to a WFPB diet as you can; the closer your food is to its natural form, the better.

10. VEGANISM FOR A HEALTHIER LIFESTYLE

Now, if you are considering becoming vegan, then you have probably spent a bit of time researching some of the health benefits of veganism. Perhaps you've read a few books, watched a couple of programmes and had a good look on the internet. Like with anything, there is a huge wealth of information out there, but there is also a staggering amount of misinformation too. This is why I thought I would include this handy little section so you can get clued up on some of the amazing benefits of being vegan. You could also memorise some of these fabulous facts in preparation for the next time that someone tries to convince you that a vegan diet is unhealthy.

The fact is, animal-products have been proven to be a cause of many diseases; many of which diseases are barely prevalent in Eastern countries, where animal-products aren't eaten anywhere near as much as in Western countries. When I first started looking into veganism properly, I was really shocked at the horrendous impact that meat-eating can have on our health and this was the biggest factor in my decision to become vegan – I wanted to improve my health and massively reduce my body's chances of becoming ill because I want to live the longest and fullest life I possibly can. So, when people talk about how they couldn't possibly be vegan because they love cheese too much, I just think about how I love my heart and arteries too much and how I would rather not fill them with cholesterol. I actually view meat-eating now a bit like smoking; smoking used to be marketed as being healthy decades ago and now everyone knows how bad it is for you – I think it's the same with animal products, but we just haven't reached the point yet where authorities have admitted to all of the scientific evidence which proves how unhealthy eating these products are.

Therefore, I have listed below a few diseases which evidence has shown are affected by the consumption of animal-products. I have tried to keep this section short and sweet because there is a wealth of information out there which I encourage you to look into if you are interested in this area of veganism – just have a look in my reference section at the end of the book to get some inspiration of which researchers, authors and doctors to look into.

Before you begin though, I normally avoid being what people call a 'pushy' vegan because people don't like to confronted about facts which are negative about their diet, but I feel like it is important for me to share a small snippet of information here on this topic. Feel free to skip it if you wish you but this is the information that made me decide to become vegan.

Arthritis

-       A study placed sufferers of osteoarthritis onto a WFPB diet, whilst the control group continued their usual meat-eating diet. The WFPB group reported significantly less pain within just two weeks of being on their new diet and greater mobility within six weeks (Clinton et al. 2015).
-       Another study found that the risk of suffering from degenerative arthritis was increased when consumption of meat

products is increased (Fraser 2006).

Asthma

- Researchers took 35 severe-asthma patients and placed them on a vegan diet. After just 4 months, 71% of the patients reported improvements, increasing to 92% after one year (Lindhal et al. 1985)
- A study found that a higher intake of fruits and vegetables helped to reduce the risk of developing asthma and reduced the symptoms of asthma and that the traditional Western diet (high in dairy and fats and low in fibre) increased asthma symptoms and worsened airway and lung function and increased inflammation (Alwarith 2020).

Cancer

- The protein casein, which is the main protein found in cow's milk, increases the growth rate of cancer cells, whereas protein from plants does not do this (Campbell and Campbell 2018).
- Having a higher fibre intake, which comes with having a higher plant-based food consumption, has been associated with lower cancer rates of the colon and rectum (Campbell and Campbell 2018).

Cholesterol

- In the enormous China Study, which studied 880 million people, they found that animal foods (such as meat, milk, eggs, fish and fats) were associated with increasing levels of blood cholesterol, whereas plant foods were associated with decreasing levels of blood cholesterol (Campbell and Campbell 2018).

-    A meta-analaysis of over 8000 studies concluded that plant-based diets were associated with lower total cholesterol, lower LDL cholesterol and lower HDL cholesterol (Barnard 2017).

Diabetes

-    After consuming cow's milk, the body can produce BSA antibodies which accidentally attack the pancreas cells, resulting in insulin production being affected and leading to type 1 diabetes (Campbell and Campbell 2018).
-    Researchers have found that WFPB diets, with no or very limited intake of animal products or refined foods, have been able to prevent and treat type 2 diabetes (McMacken 2017).

Heart Disease

-    You may have heard that the biggest risk factor for heart disease is cholesterol, specifically LDL cholesterol which deposits cholesterol into the arteries. LDL cholesterol is found in saturated fats such as in meat and junk food, trans fats such as in processed food and dairy and dietary cholesterol which is found particularly in eggs (Greger 2018). That's right, eggs are little bundles of high cholesterol, ready to help a baby chicken to grow.
-    Meat causes our body's arteries to become inflamed almost immediately after eating it due to the endotoxins which it contains that can't be broken down by cooking or the digestive processes (Greger 2018).

Osteoporosis

-    Think cow's milk gives you strong bones? Higher consumption of animal products across different countries has been

associated with higher rates of fractures (Abelow 1992)
-        Animal protein increases the blood's acidity which causes the body to try and fight it by neutralising the acidity – it does this by pulling calcium from the bones, which in turn weakens the bones and creates a higher risk of fracture (Campbell and Campbell 2018).

How Veganism Affects Our Planet

This may surprise you but eating animals doesn't just have a negative impact on our health, it is also bad for our beautiful planet. Just take a look at the startling facts below, which were quoted from the inspirational documentary Cowspiracy (which was executive-produced by Leonardo DiCaprio), an incredible programme which I absolutely recommend that you watch if you are interested in our environment.

-        Animal agriculture (the raising of livestock such as cattle for human consumption) is responsible for 18% of all greenhouse gas emissions, which is more than the combined emissions for ALL forms of transportation (cars, planes, boats, trains etc!)
-        Animal agriculture uses 34-76 TRILLION gallons of water per year, compared to fracking which uses about 70-140 billion gallons of water per year.
-        Want to save the rainforest? Up to 91% of Amazon rainforest destruction is caused by raising livestock for food.
-        Do you have a non-plastic straw to help save the ocean? The leading cause of species extinction, ocean dead zones, water pollution and habitat destruction is animal agriculture.
-        Some people say they eat fish because it's not the same as meat, but it's not just the fish that are being killed. For every pound of fish caught from the ocean, up to 5 pounds of other marine wildlife (dolphins, turtles, sharks etc) are also accidentally caught and killed. It has been estimated that around 650,00 whales, dolphins and seals are killed each

year by this fishing process.

- 82% of starving children live in countries where food is fed to animals to produce animal-products which are eaten by people in western countries. 1.5 acres of land which can produce 375 pounds of beef could produce 37,000 pounds of plant-based food.

- The land-usage required to feed a vegan for a year is 1/6th of an acre. A vegetarian uses 3x as much as a vegan and a meat-eater uses a whopping 18x as much as a vegan.

- Here is a brilliant summary: every day, one vegan person saves 1100 gallons of water, 45 pounds of grain, 30 square-feet of forested land, 20 pounds CO_2 and one animal's life.

Just think, the more and more people who stop eating animal products, the less destruction will be caused not only on our bodies but also on our planet.

11. 5 EASY STEPS TO BECOME VEGAN

Hopefully, you have reached this chapter because you've read everything previously- if not and you've just skipped straight to this chapter, then head back to the beginning and get reading! Otherwise this isn't going to make a whole lot of sense! If you have made it here through reading the rest of the book then welcome, if you have come this far then you are well on your journey to becoming vegan – yay!

So, you've read the previous chapters and hopefully becoming vegan seems a lot easier and more accessible to you now. But maybe you're wondering where to start and what to do next? Let's break it down into 5 easy steps to set you off on your journey.

1. Enlist social support

I personally think that this is a really important step because it is so much easier to achieve something when you have enrolled the support of your family and friends. I have also found that by telling someone else what I'm going to do, there is more chance that I will actually get on with it and do it – whatever it may be! I'm sure you can think of your own examples of this too. For me, one of the most important parts of my journey was when my husband and I decided together that we were both going to go vegan. If only one us had wanted to do it then I can imagine it would have been SO MUCH more difficult to do. That isn't to say that you have to convince your spouse and family to be vegans too – although it would of course be better for their health – but a little support goes a long way.

2. Decide on your 'why'

What are your reasons for becoming vegan? Perhaps it because you want to be healthier; you have an illness or disease that you want to improve through diet; you want to lose weight; you want to improve your athletic performance; you want to take a stand against animal cruelty or you want to look after your environment. Whatever your reason is, you need to identify it and remember why you started the journey. Not because you might be tempted by meat – be prepared for people to waft bacon sarnies under your nose with a smug look on their face and ask if you aren't tempted... But because this is a big and important change in your life and I often like to reflect on this important decision that I've taken to improve my health and look after my body and that's what I will say if anyone wishes to question me on my choices. Let's be honest though, you may find the first few weeks a bit tricky whilst you are learning what you can and can't eat and it might be good for you to remind yourself why you started.

3. Get rid of all animal products from your kitchen!

Once you have completed this step, you will really feel like you have taken a huge step on your journey to being vegan and it is SUPER exciting! When I completed this step, I took every food item out of my fridge, freezer and cupboards – one place at a time though of course. Then I sorted through every single piece of food and, if it didn't have any animal products in, I would put it back in the now vegan fridge or cupboard where it came from. Any products that I did find which had animal products in, I put onto the kitchen table for me to sort out at the end. When you are doing this, I think it is a really important step to empty everything out of the cupboard or part of the kitchen you are sorting – this is a minimalism technique and really helps you to see what you actually have. You also need to check everything, you would be surprised how many random things like condiments (like table sauces), biscuits, hot chocolate powders and tins of soup have some form of animal product in. When you have been through every nook and cranny of your kitchen and removed all food items containing animal products onto the kitchen table, you may end up with a rather large pile of stuff! You now have a few choices about what you can do with all of this food. Firstly, absolutely do not put it back in the cupboards to work your way through, it is so much easier to make a clean, fresh start in one hit, so we need to get rid of this food! You don't have to bin it all though; there might be some perishable items like half-used bottles of milk or butter that you might feel need to be binned. Or you can donate any items that haven't been opened to a local food bank or give it away to friends and family. For me, I gave most of my remaining food to other members of my family who don't live with us, so at least it was going to be used by someone. This is such an enormously-important step on your journey and, I think, is a very transformative and special moment. So, enjoy it!

4. Plan your meals for the first week

This step is really useful in helping to become your new life a reality and can help you to ease yourself into the world of veganism. Have another look through the recipes and meal ideas that were included earlier on in this book and make a list of a few that you would like to try. Have a think about your week ahead and consider things like how much time you will have to cook, whether you will need to make lunch to take to work and what days might you need to make a quick and easy meal. Now draw yourself up a simple plan for each day and make a note of ideas you could have for breakfast, lunch and dinner each day for the week. By the way, this isn't something that you should do every week, I just think that it is a good way to make your first week of vegan-eating less intimidating and a lot easier if you have planned ahead. Something else which I did when I was at the start of my vegan journey was to sit for an hour or so in the evening, just searching through the internet and trying to find easy recipes that I wanted to have a go at. A word of warning though, I did find that most recipes I came across seemed quite complicated even though they were labelled as 'easy' or 'beginner', but I really wasn't used to cooking anything from scratch so they may well have seemed easy to other people. So please don't feel despondent when looking up recipes, there are some really great beginner recipes out there and, with time, you will find it easier to attempt the other recipes that you come across, but for now there are always the recipes and simple meal-building ideas that you can refer back to from earlier on in this book.

5. Make your initial shopping trip

Ok, so remember those chapters earlier on where we discussed the vegan cupboard-filler items and things you would find on a vegan shopping list? Head back there and make a list of everything you need to get on your next shopping trip. I do highly recommend that you stock up on this first trip with most, if not all, of the items which I mentioned in that chapter. This includes the herbs and spices because most vegan recipes will call for a range of these to be used and, if you are anything like I was, I didn't really own any herbs and spices whatsoever! My husband actually built us a spice rack to put all of our new jars on because I was so proud of them! This first shopping trip will probably take you a bit longer that you would usually spend on your shopping because you will likely be looking in parts of the store that you may not have visited before and you will probably be spending a bit of time reading product-labels and looking for vegan versions of things. Luckily though, it is quite easy to read labels nowadays because most animal-products are listed in bold or there will be a handy label which tells you the product is vegan. You will also want to make a note of any extra ingredients that you might need for the meals that you've decided on for your first week of veganism! I found my first vegan shopping trip to be quite fun so leave yourself plenty of time to enjoy yourself and the new discoveries you will make.

And there we have it! My top five tips for making a start on your vegan journey!

OUTRO: THE END OF THE BOOK AND YOUR BEGINNING

I am so pleased that you have made it this far through the book and are clearly dedicated to the beautiful, amazing life-changing experience that is becoming a vegan. I am so excited for you to begin your journey and experience the wonderful health benefits that will be coming your way.

Thank you so much for reading this book and I really hope that it has been useful to you and has inspired you to take your first steps into becoming a vegan. I feel passionately that eliminating animal-products from the diet is possibly the single most important thing that you can do for your health and I hope that more and more lovely people like you will take the decision to lead a healthier animal-product-free lifestyle. Please share this book with your family and friends so that we can all live our best, healthiest and happiest lives.

Peace out,

Francesca x

REFERENCES

Abelow, B.J., (1992). *Cross-cultural association between animal dietary protein and hip fracture: a hypothesis.* Thesis, Yale University School of Medicine. [Online]. Available from: https://citeseerx.ist.psu.edu/viewdoc/download?doi=10.1.1.674.9378&rep=rep1&type=pdf

Alwarith, J., Barnard, M., Brandon, L., Brooks, A., Crosby, L., Kahleova, H., Levin, M. (2020). *The role of nutrition in asthma prevention and treatment.* [Online]. Available at: https://pubmed.ncbi.nlm.nih.gov/32167552/

A.U.M Films and Media (2014). *Cowspiracy* [Online]. Directed by Kip Andersen and Keegan Kuhn. Santa Rosa: A.U.M Films and Media. Available from: https://www.cowspiracy.com/

A.U.M Films and Media (2015). *What the Health* [Online]. Directed by Kip Andersen and Keegan Kuhn. Santa Rosa: A.U.M Films and Media. Available from: http://vimeo.com/ondemand/whatthehealth

Barnard, N., Levin, S., Yokoyama, Y. (2017). *Association between plant-based diets and plasma lipids: a systematic review and meta-analysis.* [Online]. Available from: https://academic.oup.com/nutritionreviews/article/75/9/683/4062197

Campbell, T.C. and Campbell, T,M. (2018). *The China study.* 2nd ed. London: Pan Books.

Clinton, C., O'Brien, S., Law, J., Renier, C., Wendt, M. (2015) *Whole-foods, plant-based diet allieviates the symptoms of osteoarthritis.* [Online]. Available from: https://www.ncbi.nlm.nih.gov/pmc/articles/PMC4359818/

Fraser, G., Hailu, A., Knutsen, S. (2006). *Associations between meat consumption and the prevalence of degenerative arthritis and soft tissue disorders in the Adventist health study, California USA.* [Online]. Available from: https://pubmed.ncbi.nlm.nih.gov/16453052/

Greger, M. (2012). How does meat cause inflammation? [Online]. Available from: https://nutritionfacts.org/2012/09/20/why-meat-causes-in-flammation/

Greger, M., (2018). *How not to die.* 2nd ed. London: Pan Books.

Greger, M. (2020). The best diet for weight loss and disease prevention. [Online]. Available from: https://nutritionfacts.org/video/the-best-diet-for-weight-loss-and-disease-prevention/

Lindahl, O., Lindwall, L., Spangberg, A., Stenram, A., Ockerman, P.A. (1985). *Vegan regimen with reduced medicationin the treatment of bronchial asthama.* [Online]. Available from: https://pubmed.ncbi.nlm.nih.gov/4019393/#:~:text=Thirty%2Dfive%20patients%20who %20had,significant%20decrease%20in%20asthma%20symptoms.

McMacken (2016). *7 things that happen when you stop eating meat.* [Online]. Available at: https://www.forksoverknives.com/wellness/7-things-that-happen-when-you-stop-eating-meat/

McMacken, M., Shah, S. (2017). *A plant-based diet for the prevention and treatment of type 2 diabetes.* [Online]. Available from: https:// www.ncbi.nlm.nih.gov/pmc/articles/PMC5466941/#:~:text=There %20is%20a%20general%20consensus,and%20treating%20type %202%20diabetes.

ACKNOWLEDGEMENT

Thank you to you for purchasing this book. I hope you enjoy your journey into veganism!

Thank you also to my lovely family who didn't disown me when I became vegan.

I couldn't end without thanking my wonderful husband, Steve, whose loving support encouraged me to make my idea for a book into a reality. So, thank you my darling.

I also want to thank my dog, just because I can (and because she's adorable and amazing).

Printed in Great Britain
by Amazon

GAY PRIDE

Craig Rodwell, founder, Oscar Wilde Bookstore, October 14, 1969.

GAY PRIDE

Photographs from Stonewall to Today

Fred W. McDarrah and Timothy S. McDarrah

Introductions by Allen Ginsberg and Jill Johnston

Historical essay by Robert Taylor

a cappella books

Note

This book is a photo documentary of people, places, and events that I have covered for the *Village Voice*, where I have been chief photographer and picture editor since 1959. In addition to the gay pride movement, I have photographed the beat generation, literary icons, Greenwich Village, New York artists, politicians, and famous personalities; some of these subjects have resulted in books. Last year, my son Patrick J. McDarrah, while cataloging my photos, suggested I should do a book on the gay pride movement to celebrate the twenty-fifth anniversary of Stonewall. He deserves credit for the idea, for inspiring me, and for acting as editorial consultant. I also want to thank my son Timothy S. McDarrah for interviewing an excellent group of men and women, gay and straight. To my wife Gloria Schoffel McDarrah, a special thanks for editing the bibliography. And finally, I am indebted to Richard Carlin of a cappella books for his good advice and guidance throughout this project.

Fred W. McDarrah
January 15, 1994

©1994 Fred W. McDarrah and Timothy S. McDarrah
San Francisco photos ©1994 by RINK FOTO
Cover design by Tim Kirkman

First edition
ISBN 1-55652-214-2
94-4994 CIP

Published by a cappella books
an imprint of Chicago Review Press, Incorporated
814 North Franklin Street
Chicago, Illinois 60610

Printed in the United States of America

5 4 3 2 1

McDarrah's Parades

Allen Ginsberg

As friend, cultural co-worker and sometime subject of Fred McDarrah and his neighborly camera I've marveled his historic constancy, decades of endurance. He's a working photographer like his eccentric Manhattan predecessor, the illustrious news pix artist, Weejee. For the *Village Voice* (radically Bohemian in its first decades), McDarrah in place focused his camera at cultural action in Manhattan hot spots—especially Greenwich Village, migrations of underground arts to Lower East Side (later commercially renamed "East Village"), & on transformations of Soho loft and gallery society.

This happened over half a century, McDarrah present, his camera flashing thru 1950s nascent subterranean counterculture, the mind-altering youth culture of the 1960s, Government blockades & psychic disillusionments of the '70s, desperate upwardly-mobile graspings for personal safety in 1980s, and return to sane tragic Earth beginning 1990s. McDarrah's photographs present a classic spectrum of themes parallel to alteration of U.S. consciousness—Anarchist street action, art openings, poetry readings, Living Theater, race drama, political spectacles, presidential conventions, folk music years, police riots, drug tribulations, underground cinema days, rock and roll studios and these Gay Liberation parades.

He's paid humble attention year after year to his beat—curious intersection of journeyman journalist & cultural archivist. He has soulful instinct for human ground under his special subjects. Though not gay, a hard laboring family man himself, he's made photo records of gay parades for decades—sign of a real artist's inquisitive sympathy, intelligent democracy.

Think of the historic importance of coming out of the closet! Stonewall's cry echoed round the world! Spiritual liberation meant gay liberation also, the liberation of individual veracity against hypocrisies of church, state, and age-old social sadism. A revelation of actuality in midst of mental hallucination and emotional repression. Truth against "lies, age-old, age-thick."

What was the fix to begin with? Legendary gay bars owned by organized crime paid off the New York police, and if they didn't they were closed down. Something went wrong with the payoffs at Stonewall Inn. So the customary repression of gay social life was motiv'd by hypocritical greed & sadism. As the sign says:

"GAY PROHIBITION CORRUPT$ COP$ AND FEED$ MAFIA"

Who rebelled against this police fraud? We see hairy chested guys with leather caps like cops, curbstone pixies on roller-skates applauding the parade, white-clad pure butch lesbians, poseurs mugging in front of Stonewall's grafitti'd facade, "Gay Cruise" billboards above Christopher Street's classic cigar-store corner, Rock Hudson elegies & T-shirt sociologies on Keith Haring's shop wall, a gay vet tombstone, Carmen Miranda banana hat clones, transvestite motorcyclists, brown skins dancing, AIDS Die-ins, Peter Orlovsky & myself musing in bed 1959, arm in arm old lovers bald, Baldwin & marble Lincoln, Auden's wrinkle-faced dignity, Gay Liz comix covers, thirtysomething male hands sharing Affidavits of Domestic Partnership, magic homosex symbols flagged above Grove Street's old brick roadway, a limp protester dragged off by cops, a "Love Boys" spray-painted door, bath-house queens and bare chest youthful cuties, Priests & Amazons, campy mitered Bishops & Gay Church floats, 1973 night crowds and balloons, Stonewall Inn shut down, a sign for "Bagels And" above its old brown brick front.

These Anniversary parades, and records thereof like Fred McDarrah's, are now significant as we approach end of millennium. Think of present circumstances—recent revelation of the tortured & torturing blackmail psyche of the mad transvestite J. Edgar Hoover in the closet—the late powerful homophobe N.Y. Cardinal Francis Spellman dallying with Broadway chorus boys on the privacy of citizen Roy Cohn's yacht! Roy Cohn himself a tax-free anti-faggot power head queer lawyer for the N.Y. Diocese, organized crime hats, androgynous politicians & macho millionaires, gay pimp for the Director of the F.B.I. How many magic Cardinals & religious fanatic priests we see unmasked, their tenderest longings hid under the iron visage of censoriousness.

This year Cardinal Spellman's successor Cardinal O'Connor still dares to put his Biblic curse on gays, no public word whispered of his famous predecessor's celebrated predilection for young men's love. Thus while Catholic Ireland herself, through miraculous legislation, presently legitimizes homosexuality, the New York Cardinal scandalously's prohibited Irish gay brigades from marching with the Green on St. Patrick's Day parades!

This degraded "Family Values" theopolitics has become a worldwide mask for mind control as against spiritual liberation. Hear the late Khomeini Ayatollah and his successor little Satans denounce "Spiritual Corruption," along with Stalin, Mao & Hitler. Listen to Pat Robertson his confrères & his guru W. A. Criswell, the fundamentalist Svengali of a "Biblical Inerrancy" cult, intolerant of any deviance from mind controlled by their interpretation of the "Good Book."

These vicious priesthoods are allied with beer magnates and tobacco Senators in hierarchies of political ambition, demagoguery, power addiction, nationalist chauvinism, military aggression, assassinations and war. Intolerant of other faiths, sexualities and folkways! Fraudulent ethical poseurs set family members against each other, & oppose ancient true family values of sympathy, tolerance, forgiveness, intimacy, humor and fidelity.

Fred McDarrah's views of the Stonewall parades present these true human values. Here we have the onlooker's inquisitiveness—What a citizen of Manhattan might see over a period of years—gay character epiphanies—A nation in spiritual transformation.

November 15, 1993
Paris

Firestorm on Christopher Street
Jill Johnston

The uprising of lesbians and gay men in late June–early July 1969 on the streets outside the Stonewall bar in Greenwich Village marks a great watershed moment in both cultural history and the lives of many citizens. I think of Stonewall myself as an event dividing time into B.C. (before consciousness) and A.D. (after death—of the life before consciousness). It was the event that catalyzed the modern gay and lesbian political movement. It changed the way thousands, ultimately millions, of men and women thought of themselves. It designated the beginning of the possibility of integrated lives for those who had lived divided against themselves—split between who they really were and what they knew they were supposed to be, between what they did and how they felt and what they said. It represented the birth of an identity unprecedented in society. Stonewall, we can see now, was surely inevitable, the launching of the last revolution in a decade of civil disruptions by all disadvantaged minorities for rights and visibility.

The foundation for the Stonewall riots had been laid by the second wave of feminism, which gathered momentum in the late '60s, and the small but growing homophile movement of the '50s and '60s. Pockets of resistance preceded

Stonewall. As the general mood of antiwar and civil rights insurgents turned mean and violent in 1968, with the assassinations of Robert F. Kennedy and Martin Luther King, Jr., the frustrations over Vietnam, the intransigence of government, the suppression of the Black Power movement through harassment, beatings, and jailings, and the cumulative rage of activist women, the possibility existed of a firestorm occurring if a single lit match was thrown into any urban location where homosexuals lived. That location turned out to be the Stonewall Inn, a gay bar that had regularly been raided by the police.

The night of June 27, 1969, for reasons that remain historically inexplicable, a small crowd on the street outside the Stonewall Inn that gathered while a police raid was in progress not only refused to disperse as it usually did but grew in numbers, and in anger, until an accumulation of small violent incidents—confrontations between police and patrons—caused the crowd to erupt in a mass action against its agents of oppression.

I happened to be in Europe at that moment, returning to New York in August. By November, I was introduced to Jim Fouratt and Lois Hart, both leaders of the new Gay Liberation Front (GLF) that had formed in the wake of Stonewall. Lois Hart and her activist friends had detected submerged lesbian ramblings in my *Village Voice* column. Indeed, since the fall of 1968 I had been writing of my travels with a young woman with the urgency and desperation of one both in love and in fear of the normal disastrous outcome for such relationships. By the time the GLF found me, I was sustaining the enraged chemistry that is thought to make a person predisposed to revolutionary ideas. Nonetheless, I was not an instant convert.

Until this time, I had lived in a state grandly oblivious to all forms of politics. I had the well-known resistance associated with assumed privileges. I had not had an easy life, but had been making my way creatively in the art world—traditionally itself a bastion against politics—for a dozen years. In 1969, I was even less conscious of being a woman than I was of my emotional/sexual identity. But once I "got it," nobody could have been more turbulently wrathful than I was—possibly because I was so belatedly political, pushing forty already. An extensive past of my own collusiveness in my devastations as a woman and a lesbian washed over me in great waves of disgust and disbelief.

Now, in the 1990s, we can look back at our progress and setbacks over the years. This book is a testimonial to a moment in time that we regard with the awe, the historicity, of an ancestral totem. Stonewall was not an event without a background, but it established the basic tenets of our revolution. Thereafter, no accommodations were to be made to the judges of our "condition," particularly of course the psychiatrists, or to the ban on visibility or self-identification that had existed forever so far as we knew. A legitimate minority had arisen, taking its place amongst women, blacks, the poor, the aged, the young, and the animals. The struggle for civil rights began right then, and continues now, in a still-hostile environment, with populations still largely determined to deny homosexuals their identity.

I see lesbians especially beleaguered in this struggle, stuck as they have been in a kind of no-man's-land between the feminists and gay men, with vital interests aligning them to each group, and with naturally the least visibility. The fortunes of lesbians since 1969 have thrown them most persuasively together with gay men in common cause. It's unfortunate, as I see it, that the lesbian constituency has not emerged as a perceived leadership of the women's movement. This is one of my hopes for the future.

I see also decades of contest for recognition and rights, often making me wish I could be thawed out at some future glorious time of true liberation.

November 15, 1993
New York City

Gay Rights in America
Robert Taylor

For the first three hundred years of America's history, the act of love between two men or two women was so abhorrent that decent people would not speak its name. Those who were brave or foolish enough to engage in this act lived shadowy lives marked by fear and self-hatred. Occasionally one of them would be caught and severely punished. But mostly they hid.

In April 1993, hundreds of thousands of gay men and lesbians—perhaps as many as a million—marched proudly through the streets of Washington, D.C., demanding their right to live their lives as they chose, openly and unafraid, free from discrimination in the jobs they could hold and the places they could live. Parents marched with their gay children. Heterosexual men and women marched in solidarity. The President of the United States met ahead of time with leaders of the march and sent a message to be read to the assembled crowd.

How did such a momentous change come about?

Early American Attitudes

As soon as the first English settlers reached the shores of North America in the early seventeenth century, they began drawing up the laws that would govern them. Of the twelve capital crimes they recognized, one was lovemaking between men. For many of the other offenses, they borrowed the language of the English common law, but for this one they went all the way back to the Old Testament: "If any man lyeth with mankind, as he lyeth with a woman, both of them have committed abomination, they both shall surely be put to death."

This formula was adopted by the colonies of Massachusetts, Connecticut, New Hampshire, New York, New Jersey, and Pennsylvania. After the American Revolution, in 1786, Pennsylvania abolished the death penalty, and other states soon followed its example. The punishment in Massachusetts became imprisonment for not more than twenty years; in New York, ten years; and in Pennsylvania, five years for a first offense, ten years for a second. Those who were forced to discuss this act, for legal or punitive reasons, generally agreed to call it sodomy. (At that time, prosecution of women was almost nonexistent, though the ban on love between them was just as strong.)

Conditions of life in America began to change as the country shifted from an overwhelmingly agricultural society to one in which capitalism played an increasingly important part. By the second half of the nineteenth century, mills and factories were pulling men, and some women, off the farms and into the industrial world, out of the small towns where everyone knew everyone else into the fast-growing cities where a person could fade into the crowd.

"Affection, intimate relationships, and sexuality moved increasingly into the realm of individual choice, seemingly disconnected from how one organized the production of goods necessary for survival," says historian John D'Emilio in his book *Sexual Politics, Sexual Communities: The Making of a Homosexual Minority in the United States 1940–1970.* "In this setting, men and women who felt a strong erotic attraction to their own sex could begin to fashion from their feeling a personal identity and a way of life."

Fundamental changes in the country's economic base were especially important for women, who in the past, except for the very wealthy, had no money of their own. Simply in order to survive, many of them had gone from a father's home to the home of a husband. If they didn't marry, they lived with a member of their family. The men who controlled society recognized, patronizingly, that women's tender emotions and sensitive natures often led them into what were called "romantic friendships" with other women. These were tolerated so long as they did not interfere with marriage and procreation. Unquestionably, at least some romantic friendships involved real love and sexual desire, but there was no way these women could ever make a life for themselves.

Two things altered that: the move of women into the workplace, and the opening up to them of higher education. "More than any other phenomenon," says historian Lillian Faderman in her book *Odd Girls and Twilight Lovers*, "education may be said to have been responsible for the spread among middle-class women of what eventually came to be called lesbianism. Not only did it bring them together in large numbers within the women's colleges, but it also permitted them literally to invent new careers such as settlement house work and various kinds of betterment professions in which they could be gainfully and productively employed and to create all-female societies around those professions."

The Scientific Study of Sex

Another change that came about late in the nineteenth and early in the twentieth centuries was a new conception of lovemaking between members of the same sex. Until then, the cultures of Europe and North America had never thought of someone who did such a thing as a distinct kind of person. These activities had always been seen as just another form of sinful or criminal behavior to which anyone might succumb. The change began with the appearance in the medical profession of a new area of study: sexology. Those who began to examine closely sexual behavior soon decided that desire between two men or two women was limited to certain individuals who could be identified and whose involuntary sexual orientation had a biological or psychological root. The new medical definition allowed sexologists to see persons who loved others of the same sex as deviants who were essentially different from other people.

Some sexologists were convinced that unnatural traits were the result of bad heredity. Because, to them, evolution was a continuing progression upward with humankind at its pinnacle, it was easy to believe that any behavior that failed to contribute to the improvement of the human race was a regression. Persons who demonstrated such behavior were "degenerate" because their genes were defective. This meant that their deviant activities had a physiological basis.

Those who preferred members of their own sex were quick to internalize these opinions. Now that they had an identity in the eyes of medical experts, there was no reason they should not have an identity in their own. And if they were born with that identity, they should not be expected to change; there was no rational excuse for punishing them, because all they were doing was simply being what they were.

In parts of Europe after the French Revolution, the Napoleonic Code had removed penalties for sexual activity between consenting adults. Several of the German states had adopted the code but, in the late 1860s, when they were unified under Prussian auspices, a provision called Paragraph 175 was proposed

Gay Pride Day, June 27, 1970.

to recriminalize sodomy in all the states. In 1869, a Hungarian doctor named Karoly Benkert (using the pseudonym K. M. Kertbeny) wrote a long open letter to the Prussian minister of justice. He coined the word "homosexual" to describe people who loved members of the same sex. He defended homosexual behavior, argued that the state had no business interfering with what went on in people's bedrooms, and called on the authorities to reject the proposed paragraph. Benkert also argued that leaving homosexuals alone would pose no threat to others because homosexuality, as the sexologists were saying, is not acquired, but innate. Benkert's efforts were ignored, and Paragraph 175 was inserted into German law in 1871. Homosexuals were once again subject to legal prosecution throughout unified Germany.

German homosexuals did not give up. In 1897, Magnus Hirschfeld founded the Scientific Humanitarian Committee. Although the organization sponsored a considerable amount of research and discussion about homosexuality and other sex-related phenomena, it concentrated its efforts on abolishing the laws against homosexual behavior. It drew up a petition that was signed by thousands of Germans, including many leading political, literary, and medical figures of the day—but to no avail.

In 1919, Hirschfeld opened the Institute for Sexual Research in Berlin, and the Scientific Humanitarian Committee moved into offices on the second floor. The two independent organizations continued their activities until the spring of 1933. Then, on the morning of May 6, about a hundred Nazi students from a nearby school gathered outside the institute. They smashed down the doors, vandalized the building, and loaded their trucks with more than 10,000 books from the institute's library and boxes of papers from research files. A few days after the raid, the books and papers were piled on the square in front of the Berlin Opera House and burned. The world's first fledgling movement for homosexual rights came to an abrupt end.

During these years, although some in America were aware of what was happening in Germany, there was almost no organized activity among homosexuals in the United States. The one person speaking openly on the subject was Emma Goldman. In an article for the Scientific Humanitarian Committee's 1923 *Yearbook*, Goldman said, "It is a tragedy, I feel, that people of a different sexual type are caught in a world which shows so little understanding for homosexuals, is so crassly indifferent to the various gradations and variations of gender and their great significance in life."

In 1924, influenced by the activities in Germany, a group of homosexuals in Chicago established the Society for Human Rights to "combat the public prejudices" against homosexuality. The following year, however, the wife of one of the organizers notified the police, and four members of the group were arrested and hauled off to jail. That put an end to the society, and no other organizations were established until after World War II.

At some point, while the conception of homosexuality was changing, so too did the terminology. For many of those to whom it was applied, the word "homosexual" put too much emphasis on sexual activity as a defining characteristic. While it might be all right as an overall classification, it did not allow for the fact that the people it described were more than what they did in bed. The word "gay," originally applied to prostitutes in the last part of the nineteenth century, had, by the first half of the twentieth, come to be applied to homosexuals. It became the accepted term for homosexual men. For convenience, "gay" would often be used to refer to both male and female homosexuals, but many women preferred to be called lesbians.

The Liberating Effect of Wartime

The Second World War brought a major upheaval to American life as millions of men and women were mobilized to take part in the war effort. Large numbers of the country's young people left the isolation of small towns and ever-watchful families to spend twenty-four hours a day with others of the same sex, whether in the armed forces or on the assembly lines. There were those who had already recognized their homosexuality and merely took advantage of opportunities that came their way. Others had no idea before and woke up to something they had never realized about themselves.

"The sex-segregated nature of the armed forces raised homosexuality closer to the surface for all military personnel," says John D'Emilio, "Army canteens witnessed men dancing with one another, an activity that in peacetime subjected homosexuals to arrest. Crowded into port cities, men on leave or those waiting to be shipped overseas shared beds in YMCAs and slept in each other's arms in parks or in the aisles of movie theaters that stayed open to house them. . . . In this setting, gay men could find one another without attracting undue attention and perhaps even encounter sympathy and acceptance by their heterosexual fellows."

The severe manpower shortage made the military more or less tolerant of gay men so long as they were discreet, but those caught having sex with another man usually found themselves in serious trouble. Army regulations clearly stated that because homosexuality was an "undesirable habit or trait of character," it was sufficient grounds for separation.

"The identification of homosexuality in the female services," says John Costello in his book *Virtue Under Fire*, "was complicated because demonstrations of physical affection were considered socially acceptable among women." Costello quotes a 1943 pamphlet for WAC officers that said "every person is born with a bisexual nature" and urged officers to distinguish between the "active homosexual," who should be "discharged as promptly as possible," and the female soldier "who has gravitated toward homosexual practices" because of the new close association with women, loneliness, or "hero worship." A transfer, a move to another barracks, or a talk with the post surgeon were suggested as remedies.

When the war was over, all leniency came to a halt. Thousands of gay and lesbian personnel were loaded on "queer ships" and sent with "undesirable" discharges to the nearest U.S. port. Many of them were afraid to go home and face their disgrace, so they stayed in the ports where they disembarked. Ironically, in this way the military contributed to the establishment of large gay and

"Jane Jones," a Los Angeles women's bar in 1942 from the Paris Poirier film, *Last Call at Maud's*; note two enlisted WACs in uniform.

lesbian enclaves in port cities such as Boston, New York, San Francisco, and Los Angeles.

Dr. Kinsey and Senator McCarthy

Soon after the end of the war, in 1948, Dr. Alfred Kinsey's report on *Sexual Behavior in the Human Male* stunned the country by revealing how widespread homosexual experience was among American men. His most startling findings were these: "37 percent of the total male population has at least some overt homosexual experience to the point of orgasm between adolescence and old age"; "10 percent of the males are more or less exclusively homosexual for at least three years between the ages of 16 and 55"; "8 percent of the males are exclusively homosexual for at least three years between the ages of 16 and 55"; and "4 percent of the white males are exclusively homosexual throughout their lives, after the onset of adolescence." How much the wartime experiences of so many men had contributed to the size of these percentages is impossible to say.

Five years later, in his 1953 book *Sexual Behavior in the Human Female*, Kinsey reported that "homosexual responses had occurred in about half as many females as males, and contacts which had proceeded to orgasm had occurred in about a third as many females as males. Moreover, compared with the males, there were only about a half to a third as many of the females who were, in any age period, primarily or exclusively homosexual." The numbers, though smaller than among males, still revealed significant lesbian activity.

In the aftermath of the war, many Americans were uncomfortable with the changes sweeping the country. Kinsey's figures underscored that "family values" were changing; some Americans took this to be proof that prohibitions against illicit sexual conduct had broken down completely and that immediate action was imperative. At the forefront of the movement against homosexuals and other "anti-American" groups was Senator Joseph McCarthy. In 1950, persecution of homosexuals began in earnest, with McCarthy leading the way. By April of that year, ninety-one homosexuals had been fired from the State Department alone, and for the next three years, gays and lesbians were dismissed from government jobs at the rate of forty to sixty a month. In 1954, the Senate finally gathered up the courage to censure Senator McCarthy, but the atmosphere of suspicion and intolerance he had helped create lasted well into the next decade. Homosexuals both inside the government and out continued to be persecuted.

Laws enacted by state legislatures and local governing bodies allowed antigay crusaders in many American towns and cities to begin closing down bars that catered to "sex perverts," both male and female. Police departments rounded up dozens, sometimes hundreds, of those they found in these bars.

Slowly but surely, a few—a very few—gays and lesbians began to organize. In 1950, some gay men formed the Mattachine Society in Los Angeles. Chapters soon opened in other cities, including Berkeley and San Francisco. In 1955, a group of eight lesbians in San Francisco founded the Daughters of Bilitis. Both organizations were far more interested in accommodation than confrontation. Mattachine sought to "educate" people so that they would drop their prejudices against homosexuals, and one of the stated objectives of the Daughters of Bilitis was "advocating a mode of behavior and dress acceptable to society." All through the 1950s, the "homophile" movement, as they called themselves, continued to be small and weak. The total membership of both the Daughters of Bilitis and the Mattachine Society in San Francisco was probably never more than two hundred.

The 1960s brought to America a mood of restlessness and militant activism. Lunch counter sit-ins, freedom rides, and marches to end racial injustice dominated the news. Not surprisingly, this new spirit infected the gay movement as well. Spearheading the new militancy among gays was Franklin Kameny, who, although he had a Ph.D. in astronomy from Harvard, was barred from government employment simply because he was a homosexual. Outraged, he and a friend organized the Mattachine Society of Washington, D.C., in 1961. As its

On April 21, 1966, members of the Mattachine Society staged a "sip-in" at Julius's Bar, 159 W. 10th Street, New York, demanding that, as open homosexuals, they be served. Liquor laws at the time forbade serving gays. Ironically, Julius's later became a gay bar. L to r: John Timmins, Dick Leitsch, Craig Rodwell, Randy Wicker.

president, Kameny led the group into battle against the federal government. There was no room on Kameny's agenda for patient pleading. "In a democracy, a private citizen is more exalted than any office holder," he maintained. "We have the right to have our grievances heard." More than that, he said, "We owe apologies to no one—society and its official representatives owe us apologies for what they have done and are doing to us."

The Washington Mattachine Society aimed its fire, in particular, at the policies of the U.S. Civil Service Commission, the separation of homosexuals from the armed forces, and the blanket denial of security clearances to all homosexuals by the Pentagon. The group persuaded the American Civil Liberties Union to support its efforts, and in August 1964, the ACLU adopted a resolution condemning the exclusion of homosexuals from governmental service as "discriminatory," calling on the federal government to "end its policy of rejection of all homosexuals."

At the same time, Randy Wicker created a one-man organization called the Homosexual League of New York and used it as a base from which to launch a media campaign. He appeared on radio programs and gave interviews to news-papers and magazines, spreading widely his appeal for gay rights.

In San Francisco, political activity took a fascinating turn. José Sarria, an entertainer at a gay bar called the Black Cat, presented satirical drag operas on Sunday afternoons that attracted huge crowds. In 1961, at the height of another of the city's frequent police crackdowns on gay bars, Sarria decided he would run for city supervisor. Although he received only about seven thousand votes, his candidacy electrified the patrons of the bars. Many of them began to think about homosexuality in political terms for the first time.

During Sarria's campaign, a group of gay men started publishing and hand-ing out a biweekly newspaper at the local bars. In it, they pointed out to gays the advantages of voting as a bloc and encouraged gays to register and vote. Before long, candidates for public office in San Francisco were buying ads in this paper. In 1966, the Daughters of Bilitis scheduled a series of public forums at which officials from several of San Francisco's municipal departments discussed gay and lesbian concerns. Candidates' nights, jointly sponsored by all of the city's gay and lesbian groups, became annual events, with attendance sometimes reaching five hundred.

Stonewall

Some of the more militant organizations, like the Homophile Action League, thought these activities were far too tame and conventional. They advocated aggressive, face-to-face confrontations, but there were still very few gays and lesbians willing to go along with that kind of approach. A catalyst was needed to inspire the rest.

On a Friday night, June 27, 1969, shortly before midnight, New York police from Manhattan's Sixth Precinct raided the Stonewall Inn, a Greenwich Village gay bar. This was the third recent raid on gay bars in the area, but this time the response was different. The two hundred or so patrons did not just run away, or quietly allow themselves to be arrested, as they had done in the past. Instead, they stood and jeered, and soon their numbers doubled, then tripled. Before the night was over, four policemen had been hurt as rioters threw coins, paving stones, cans, bottles, and even uprooted parking meters at them. The riots continued the following night, when about four hundred policemen ended up battling a crowd of more than two thousand.

The Mattachine Action Committee responded with a flier on June 29 calling for organized resistance, and by the end of July New York gays and lesbians had formed the Gay Liberation Front. Soon, GLF members were picketing airlines that

The success of the Stonewall rebellion is jubilantly celebrated outside the Stonewall Inn over the entire weekend of June 27, 1969.

had antigay employment practices and the offices of newspapers and magazines that printed demeaning articles about gay people.

In June 1970, about ten thousand gays and lesbians marched up New York's Sixth Avenue to Central Park to mark the first anniversary of the Stonewall Rebellion. Similar parades took place in Los Angeles and Chicago.

The movement spread rapidly across the country, and gay organizations proliferated. The Gay Activists Alliance, which broke away from GLF, was followed by the National Gay Task Force, later renamed the National Gay and Lesbian Task Force. By the middle of the 1970s, gay liberation groups—more than one thousand of them—had been formed in every major city and on large college campuses in the United States. They began putting pressure on state legislatures, school boards and administrators, newspapers, television stations, and churches. They turned out tens of thousands of people for demonstrations. A gay liberation press—with publications based in Los Angeles, San Francisco, Detroit, New York, and Boston—kept these widely scattered organizations aware of each other's activities.

Lesbians who helped found the gay liberation movement, however, soon realized that the overwhelming majority of its members were gay men preoccupied with their own concerns and pretty much unaware of the special concerns of lesbians, such as equal opportunity in employment and violence against women. In the early 1970s, some lesbians left the gay liberation movement for the women's movement. Others, who found as much antigay prejudice in the women's movement as they had found sexism in the gay movement, formed organizations of their own: Radicalesbians in New York, the Furies Collective in Washington, D.C., and Gay Women's Liberation in San Francisco.

One byproduct of gay liberation was the expansion of businesses and services aimed specifically at gays and lesbians. Before long, most major cities in the United States had gay and lesbian restaurants, boutiques, health clinics, counseling services, lawyers, doctors, and life insurance agents. Lesbian and gay entrepreneurs founded record companies and publishing houses, set up travel agencies, and built vacation resorts. They started literary journals, theater companies, and film collectives.

Perhaps even more important than these external changes, though, were the internal ones. Gay activism helped homosexuals stop thinking of themselves as individual victims and start seeing themselves as part of a large community, a minority on a par with the country's ethnic groups. It showed them that they could fight back and stop letting others define who they were and what they could do. And, says Lillian Faderman, it allowed them to conclude that it was

Travel agency billboard advertising gay cruises, Sheridan Square, October 31, 1990.

society that was sick, not lesbians and gays. Therefore, it was homophobia, not homosexuality, that needed to be cured.

Official changes came quickly. The American Sociological Association passed a no-discrimination resolution in 1969; the states of Connecticut, Colorado, and Oregon decriminalized sodomy in 1971; and in 1973, the U.S. Civil Service Commission eliminated its ban on the employment of lesbians and gays. Also in 1973, the American Psychiatric Association removed homosexuality from its list of mental disorders. During the 1970s, more than half the states repealed their sodomy laws, and several dozen municipalities passed antidiscrimination statutes. National politicians declared their support for gay rights.

Gay Pride Day or Gay Freedom Day parades, usually held the last Sunday in June to commemorate the Stonewall Rebellion, became annual events in cities and towns across the United States. Through the years, the numbers of participants and spectators grew to hundreds of thousands in New York and more than half a million in San Francisco. The mayors of cities as diverse as Ann Arbor, MI, and Washington, D.C., began proclaiming official Gay Pride Weeks. In 1988, a San Francisco mayor, Art Agnos, rode in a Gay Pride parade for the first time, and in

The Gay Liberation Front marching on Gay Pride Day, June 28, 1970.

1990, lavender spotlights lit up the Empire State Building in New York for three days in honor of Gay Pride Week.

The decades of the '70s and the '80s, though, were a time of an intense tug of war. Gay rights would make progress in one area, only to be beaten back in another. In 1974, Elaine Noble was elected to the Massachusetts House of Representatives, the first openly gay state legislator in the United States. In 1976, Jean O'Leary, coordinator of the National Gay Task Force, became the first openly gay delegate to the Democratic National Convention. In November 1977, Harvey Milk, a openly gay candidate, was elected to the post of city supervisor in San Francisco.

But, in June 1977, a six-month-old gay-rights ordinance in Florida's Dade County was overturned by a huge electoral margin—202,000 to 83,000. The next year, similar ordinances were voted down in St. Paul, MN, Wichita, KS, and Eugene, OR. By the time the wave reached California, it appeared to be unstoppable.

John Briggs, a state senator from Orange County, organized a statewide ballot initiative that called for the dismissal from California's schools of all openly gay teachers as well as anyone who "advocates, solicits, imposes, encourages, or

Announcing the formation of the National Gay Task Force, October 15, 1973. L to r: Ron Gold, Frank Kameny, Dr. Howard Brown, Bruce Voeller, Nathalie Rockhill. Former health administrator Brown was the first New York City official to come out.

promotes" homosexual activity. More than thirty gay and lesbian organizations sprang up across the state to fight the initiative. Some took the cautious approach of appealing for sympathy, but others relied on public demonstrations and confrontations with Briggs's supporters at every opportunity. In November 1978, California voters rejected the Briggs proposition by 58 to 42 percent. That same day, voters in Seattle chose to keep their gay-rights law by a margin of 63 to 37 percent. The wave, if not stopped, had at least been slowed.

Less than three weeks later, however, in San Francisco, Mayor George Moscone and gay city supervisor Harvey Milk were assassinated by a former policeman and city supervisor, Dan White, who resented the prominence of gays within the city. At White's trial in May 1979, he was found guilty of manslaughter, the lightest possible penalty, sparking a riot in which eleven police cars were set on fire and windows at City Hall were smashed. The clear message of the riot was that San Francisco's gay community was determined not to relinquish its hard-won political power.

During the next few years, gays and lesbians moved to the inner circles of political life in San Francisco. Many elected officials hired liaisons to the gay community; others put gay political leaders on their staffs. Gays and lesbians were elected to some of the city's lower-level positions, and others were appointed to municipal regulatory boards.

By the mid-'80s, several cities—among them Laguna Beach, CA, Key West, FL, and Bunceton, MO—had elected openly gay mayors. In a 1984 election in West Hollywood, CA, gays and lesbians were chosen to fill a majority of the positions on the city council, and lesbian activist Valerie Terrigno became mayor. New York City's mayor's office established a liaison to the gay and lesbian community. Other elected officials—the Manhattan district attorney, the city council president, and the controller—all set up similar liaisons in the 1980s. An open lesbian joined the advisory committee for the sex equity task force of the city's board of education, and any group that discriminated against homosexuals lost its funding from the city.

Even the police departments in a number of large cities began to recruit and hire lesbian and gay officers. Atlanta, Baltimore, Boston, Detroit, Los Angeles, New York, Phoenix, and San Francisco all added homosexuals to their police forces. Ironically, New York City's Sixth Precinct, from which the raid on the Stonewall Inn was launched in 1969, now has several gay and lesbian officers on its staff.

Then, once again, the pendulum swung the other way. In 1986, the U.S. Supreme Court decided, in the case of *Bowers v. Hardwick*, that the state of Georgia's law against sodomy did not violate the fundamental rights of homosexuals. Justice Harry Blackmun dissented—eloquently and forcefully—saying that "the right of an individual to conduct intimate relationships in the intimacy of his or her home seems to me to be the heart of the Constitution's protection of privacy." He said that he hoped the court would soon conclude "that depriving individuals of the right to choose for themselves how to conduct their intimate relationships poses a far greater threat to the values most deeply rooted in our Nation's history than tolerance of nonconformity could ever do."

The Impact of AIDS

In the midst of all this activity, the gay community was hit by an unexpected and horrifying crisis: AIDS. A small note published in the medical press in 1981 gave the first indication that a new disease had appeared. It spread rapidly through the country's gay population. By 1982, 471 cases had been identified in the United States; by 1985, more than 15,000; and by 1987, more than 45,000. In the last decade, 230,000 Americans—65 percent of them gay men—have been diagnosed with full-blown AIDS. Of those, more than 150,000 have already died. As many as a million more may be infected.

The arrival of AIDS gave a new urgency to political activity throughout the gay community. In each place where large numbers of cases were diagnosed, organizations sprang up to deal with the needs of the sick. Some groups offered assistance to people with AIDS, while others lobbied for better treatment and more money for research. Lesbians, who were for the most part unaffected by the disease itself, responded to the emergency by the thousands.

After a decade of losing friends to AIDS and being attacked by opponents at every turn, a weary and disheartened gay community found new hope in the candidacy of Bill Clinton. In the spring of 1992, Clinton appeared at a gay-rights fund-raising event in Los Angeles, the first time a national candidate had ever done so. "I have a vision," he told the cheering crowd, "and you're a part of it."

In his formal position papers, Clinton pledged to sign an executive order ending the U.S. military policy of barring homosexuals from serving, to support legislation to amend federal civil-rights laws to include sexual orientation, to appoint gays and lesbians to important positions in his administration, and to launch a massive effort to find a cure for AIDS.

Gay and lesbian supporters responded by raising $3.5 million for Clinton's campaign and working hard to register voters and get them to the polls. The Human Rights Campaign Fund, the nation's largest gay political lobby, with sixty thousand members, sent volunteers to six important states to round up gay votes for Clinton. These efforts paid off. Exit polls showed that nearly 75 percent of gays and lesbians voted for Clinton.

Another organization, the Gay and Lesbian Victory Fund, was set up in 1991 specifically to help finance the campaigns of openly gay and lesbian candidates. In 1992, the group raised hundreds of thousands of dollars for twelve state and local candidates, half of whom won. Just ten years ago, there were only a few openly lesbian and gay elected officials throughout the country. Now, there are seventy-five, including two long-term members of Congress, Representatives Barney Frank and Gerry Studds, both Democrats from Massachusetts, and about a dozen state legislators, one of whom, Allan Spear, is president of the Minnesota state senate. The rest are in lower-level county and municipal positions.

Pleasure over Clinton's election was tempered by the passage in Colorado of a referendum prohibiting the state from enacting laws to bar discrimination against homosexuals. The measure, approved by a margin of 54 to 46 percent, rescinded gay-rights laws already in place in the cities of Denver, Boulder, and Aspen. However, a judge on the Denver District Court immediately issued an order stopping the amendment from taking effect. In July, the Colorado Supreme

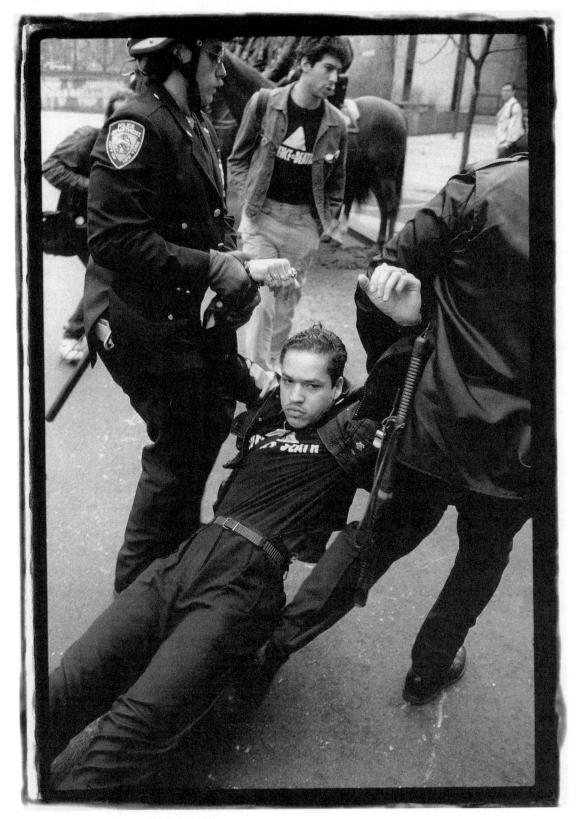

Act-Up demonstration for AIDS housing at New York's City Hall, March 28, 1989.

Court upheld the injunction, stating that the law was in violation of the equal protections clause of the U.S. constitution; at the time, Colorado's Attorney General had not decided whether to appeal the ruling to the U.S. Supreme Court.

That same election day brought happier news from Oregon, where voters defeated—56 to 44 percent—a measure that would have amended the state's constitution to classify homosexuality as "abnormal, wrong, unnatural, or perverse" and have required the state government to take steps to discourage it.

Activists argue that votes like this—some for gay rights, some against—demonstrate the need for a national statute that would override actions by individual states. Federal legislation being drafted by two Democrats, Senator Edward Kennedy and Representative Henry Waxman, would extend to gays and lesbians the same civil rights protections that are already in place for blacks, women, ethnic and religious minorities, and disabled people.

Opponents of gay rights and worried politicians have seized on the results of a recent study that reported only 1.1 percent of the men surveyed said they had been exclusively homosexual during the previous ten years. Fewer gays and lesbians would mean, theoretically, fewer votes and less political power. A Harris poll published in 1993, however, quoted a 4.4 percent figure, about the same as Kinsey's earlier estimate.

The President's Promises

President Clinton has begun to keep some of his campaign promises. He has appointed more than thirty gay men and lesbians to important positions in his administration. Two assistant secretaries, Bruce Lehman at Commerce and Roberta Achtenberg at Housing and Urban Development, are the highest-ranking openly gay or lesbian federal officials in the nation's history.

Another of Clinton's promises—that he would change the policy that keeps homosexuals from serving in the military—created an uproar throughout the country.

Before 1982, no one was questioned about sexual orientation prior to joining the armed services, but the military generally discharged people who were found engaging in homosexual activity or who exhibited "homosexual tendencies." In 1982, the Department of Defense issued a directive that said "homosexuality is incompatible with military service" and "adversely affects the ability of the military services to maintain discipline, good order, and morale." It directed that persons who wanted to join the military must be asked their sexual preference. Anyone who acknowledged being gay or lesbian would be barred from serving, and any gay or lesbian found serving in the military would be discharged.

It has been an expensive policy. The General Accounting Office says the Pentagon spent about $270 million between 1980 and 1990 finding nearly seventeen thousand homosexuals, discharging them, and replacing them. Some of those discharged had been given consistently outstanding performance reports by their superiors. Lesbians have been hit especially hard. Of all those separated from the Marine Corps, for example, a woman is seven times more likely than a man to have been removed for homosexuality.

After the election, Clinton restated his intention to lift the military ban. Protests came immediately from all directions: the Joint Chiefs of Staff; religious groups; influential members of Congress; and aroused citizens, who voiced their opposition on the country's radio and television talk shows and jammed telephone switchboards at the White House and the Capitol.

Faced with such loud and forceful opposition, President Clinton decided to implement the change more slowly than he had originally intended. He asked former Defense Secretary Les Aspin to consult with the military on the practical effects of the proposed change, then submit by July 15, 1993, a draft executive order that would end the present policy. The Senate Armed Services Committee later held a series of hearings on the matter.

"The issue," Clinton said, "is not whether there should be homosexuals in the military; everyone concedes that there are. The issue is whether men and women who can and have served with real distinction should be excluded from military service solely on the basis of their status. I believe they should not." In the end, Clinton forged a compromise with more conservative members of the military and the Congress: the military would "not ask" a person's sexual orientation and that person could serve as long as she or he did "not tell" that they were lesbian or gay. The legality of this compromise has since been questioned in the courts.

Since the early '90s, gay and lesbian leaders had been planning a march in Washington, D.C., to take place in April 1993. The fact that it coincided with the uproar over the military ban was a happy coincidence.

Although he said he would not attend the march, President Clinton continued to express support. On April 16, a week before the march, he met at the White House for more than an hour with leaders of gay and lesbian organizations. One leader, Urvashi Vaid, called the meeting "historic, the first of its kind in the Oval Office."

On April 25, members of the gay community and their supporters gathered in Washington, D.C., for what many observers called the largest demonstration ever held in the nation's capital. Its purposes were to mobilize support for ending the ban on gays in the military, to secure more funding for AIDS care and

The March on Washington for Lesbian, Gay, and Bi Equal Rights and Liberation, April 25, 1993.

research, and to win passage of legislation that would ban discrimination against gays, lesbians, and bisexuals. In recent years, the realization has taken hold that being bisexual is different from, and in some ways even more complicated than, being gay or lesbian. Bisexuals have formed groups to deal with their special concerns, and the march on Washington included them in its title and its agenda.

Organizers of the march say they met their goal of one million demonstrators. The figure given out by the U.S. Park Police was 300,000; other estimates hover around 750,000. Whatever the actual number may have been, the crowd was enormous. Marchers waited for hours to begin their walk. The march itself, which started about noon, lasted until nearly 7 P.M.

President Clinton sent a letter that was read to the demonstrators massed on the Mall. "I stand with you in the struggle for equality for all Americans," Clinton said, "including gays and lesbians." He urged the country to "put aside what divides us and focus on what we share."

Representative Gerry Studds, the openly gay congressman from Massachusetts, said after the march, "The biggest change is not in Congress, but in the people who participated. They left transformed: proud and self-respecting. In the end, that's what will make for true political power."

Now that the march is over, gays and lesbians are left wondering what the future will bring. They know that heterosexual Americans continue to have deeply ambivalent feelings about homosexuality. In some ways, disapproval is receding, and in some ways it remains strong. A 1987 poll, for example, found that 59 percent of those surveyed believed that gays and lesbians should have equal job opportunities. By the fall of 1992, that percentage had risen to 78. But, in the same 1992 poll, only 41 percent said homosexuality was "an acceptable alternative lifestyle"; 53 percent said no.

More than 130 cities and counties now have ordinances, laws, or executive orders that protect gays and lesbians from discrimination. Seven states and the District of Columbia have gay-rights laws in force, and about a dozen other states are considering such legislation. However, determined opponents in at least seven states are rounding up support for antigay measures like the one approved by Colorado voters in 1992. And twenty-four states still outlaw homosexual sodomy.

Even so, gays and lesbians are well aware of how far they have come since the old days of fear and invisibility. It seems possible that at long last they may be close to achieving their goal.

And what is it they are seeking, after all?

Andrew Sullivan, the openly gay editor of *The New Republic* magazine, says what "most gay men and women hope for" is "not the approval of anything we do in private, not the embracing of some mythical abstraction called the gay life style, not the derogation of traditional values, but merely the recognition that we are human beings too, that the mere statement of our identity should not be a cause for violence or hatred or public discrimination."

"Rocks through windows don't open doors."   —*Randy Wicker, Mattachine Society*

The Stonewall riots started on Friday night, June 27, and ended Monday morning with breaks in between for a victory celebration. The chalked message on the wall says, "To fight for our country, they invaded our rights."

After World War II, many gay men and lesbians settled in Greenwich Village. Traditionally an artistic community, the Village offered gays an opportunity to form supportive social networks. They frequented the saloons along MacDougal Street, went to the beaches at Cherry Grove and Riis Park, and pretty much kept to themselves. Still, they were always at risk of being found out at their jobs or by their families. Early on, these social networks began taking political form and, by the late '50s, the Mattachine Society and the Daughters of Bilitis encouraged gays and lesbians to deal with the prejudice against homosexuals. Taking a cue from the antiwar, civil rights, and feminist movements, gays demanded equal rights. They did not want to be harassed any more; they wanted to be heard and respected. The single incident that marked the birth of the modern gay and lesbian movement was the Stonewall Inn rebellion on the weekend of June 27, 1969.

The Stonewall Inn at 53 Christopher Street was a speakeasy during prohibition, later a restaurant catering to weddings and banquets, and then a gay bar. Saloons serving homosexuals were denied liquor licenses in those years, and it was illegal for gays to gather anywhere. Gay bars paid off the police to stay open, but many were harassed anyway because they operated without licenses; police could close them down at will. The Stonewall's kickbacks to the local cops and their Mafia vendors was reported to be $2,000 a week, but the bar took in nearly $12,000 every weekend.

The raid on the Stonewall was made by two cops, two undercover agents, and two policewomen who went inside to "observe the illegal sale of alcohol." Once inside, the detectives called the Sixth Precinct on a pay phone for backup, and the arrival of the additional cops set off the incident. Patrons were herded out of the bar while cops, headed by Deputy Inspector Seymour Pike, were pelted by gays throwing everything they could find. Thirteen people were arrested. In the course of the raid, all the mirrors, jukeboxes, phones, toilets, and cigarette machines were smashed. Even the sinks were stuffed and overflowing.

To everyone's surprise, the patrons fought back, creating an unstoppable movement of gay pride. The *Village Voice* was the only New York paper to cover the event, with Howard Smith writing from the inside and Lucian Truscott IV reporting from the outside; Truscott wrote that "Sheridan Square this weekend looked like something from a William Burroughs novel as the sudden specter of 'Gay Power' erected its brazen head and spat out a fairy tale the likes of which the area has never seen." Within a month after the riots, gays, tired of being

Stonewall

The Stonewall Inn was a quiet, little-known restaurant located near the *Village Voice* when this photo was taken on May 1, 1966; a two-story building on the corner, the Duplex Cabaret, now covers the sign painted on the brick wall.

humiliated, exploited by the Mafia, and constantly bullied by the police, closed down the Stonewall Inn. The location has since become a men's clothing store, Chinese restaurant, bagel shop, and another saloon, and in 1989, the second Stonewall sign was removed from the building. Today, the bar once again has risen from the dead as a reminder of its glorious past, with a simple neon sign in the window.

The windows of the Stonewall were boarded up with plywood and painted black after the riots. Members of the Mattachine Society as well as irate customers covered the windows with graffiti. The top statement refers to the fact that cops took payoffs from members of the mob who operated the illegal gay bars. Photographs taken over the weekend of June 27, 1969.

Inside the Stonewall Inn after the riots, the weekend of June 27, 1969.

"My life would have been completely different if [Stonewall] hadn't happened. If I grew up without an outspoken gay movement who I am as a person would have been totally different."
—Donna Minkowitz, Village Voice *reporter*

Damaged vending machine after the riots, the weekend of June 27, 1969.

On Gay Pride Day, June 30, 1974, Mama-Jean Devente (l) and a friend attach a bouquet at the Stonewall doorway to commemorate the fifth anniversary of the riots.

Actor Quentin Crisp rides in the lead car in the Gay Pride Day parade, June 27, 1982, as it passes in front of the old Stonewall Inn. Behind him are marching members of Congregation Beth Simchat Torah, New York's gay synagogue.

"I was riding in a car and I was accompanied the whole way by two policemen with faces like stone. . . . I was astounded, really, at how mild the reception for the parade was. People shouted a bit, but not much else. New York has a very Italianate element and Italians love a parade. I bet when they got home late and someone asked them where they were, they said 'a parade.' And when mama asked a parade of what, they said 'I don't even know.'"
— *Quentin Crisp*

A new Stonewall was opened in the late '80s, but it closed down on October 11, 1989, when this sign was removed.

Reborn again just before this photo was taken on October 26, 1993, 53 Christopher Street enjoys its third life simply as Stonewall, with a neon sign in the window.

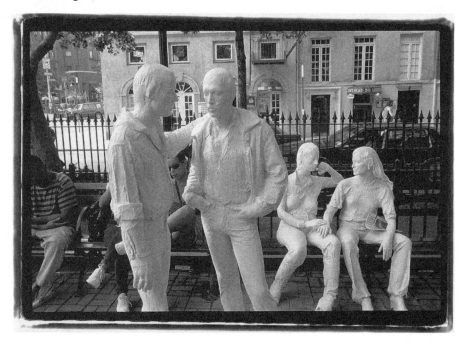

George Segal plaster sculpture, July 6, 1992, installed in Sheridan Square Park, depicts gay and lesbian couples to commemorate the 1969 Stonewall riots.

Exactly one month after Stonewall on July 27, 1969, the Mattachine Society and the Daughters of Bilitis organized the first mass rally for gay rights. Starting in Washington Square Park, fewer than two hundred openly gay men and lesbians assembled. The rally started with the distribution of lavender ribbons and armbands that apparently many were reluctant to wear. Martha Shelley, from the Daughters of Bilitis, an experienced antiwar protester at the Democratic National Convention in 1968, stood on the fountain rim and greeted her brothers and sisters, as reported in the *Village Voice*: "We're tired of being harassed and persecuted. If a straight couple can hold hands in Washington Square [park], why can't we? . . . We're tired of straight people who are hung up on sex; tired of flashlights and peeping-tom vigilantes; tired of marriage laws which punish you for lifting your head off the pillow. Socrates was a homosexual; Michelangelo was homosexual; Walt Whitman and Richard the Lion-Hearted were homosexuals."

Marty Robinson from the Mattachine Society continued with "Let me tell you homosexuals, we've got to get organized; we've got to stand up." He then led the protest march to Sheridan Square Park, where residents along West 4th Street gaped in astonishment. Nothing like this had ever been done before. Gay power, with banners waving and fists flying, had surfaced. This was only the beginning.

1969 March

Parading down West 4th Street, July 27, 1969.

Marty Robinson told the assembled crowd that "Gay power is here. . . . There are one million homosexuals in New York . . . we will not permit another reign of terror," July 27, 1969.

"I was there [at Stonewall]—I walked by earlier in the day before anything had happened. I didn't even know it was a gay bar. I was closeted at the time. No one knew at the time that it was a watershed event. I got involved some months later when a bar called The Snake Pit got raided in February 1970. There were 187 people arrested and an Argentinean named Diego Vinales jumped from the police precinct window and killed himself.

"I was the vice president of a group called the Gay Activists Alliance. There was also the Gay Liberation Front. Those groups pretty closely parallel Act-Up and Queer Nation. I think that after the quiet of the late '70s things picked up again in the early 1980s in large part because of AIDS.

"The real issue is that we've made ourselves visible and real. That was the first challenge. When we first appeared as a minority group it wasn't legitimate. Color or ethnicity was valid, but sex didn't count."
—*Arnie Kantrowitz, professor, College of Staten Island*

Jim Owles (center with kerchief), leader of the Gay Activists Alliance, urging the crowd to petition city council members to support gay rights and a fair employment practices bill, July 27, 1969.

Sheridan Square Park, July 27, 1969.

In contrast to the Stonewall riots a month earlier, only one patrolman was assigned to this march; he is shown here warning Marty Robinson not to incite the crowd, July 27, 1969.

"When I first came out, my love life took place in men's rooms and basements. Suddenly, when I came out and many others did, I had hundreds of friends. Just like anyone else."
—*Arnie Kantrowitz*

"I came to New York in the early '60s to be a bohemian/beatnik artist. I found the Actors Studio, Lee Strasberg, Greenwich Village, jazz, mary jane, gay bars, drag queens, Andy Warhol, the Judson Church performers, the Living Theater, the Caffè Cino and La Mama, civil rights marches and sit ins, the Open Theater, Communists, poetry, dirty old men, Lenny Bruce, rich people, and my first real boyfriend (Franklin Spodak). The decade moved fast. I went from a Max's Kansas City scenester, Hearst *Eye* magazine columnist, and Broadway and TV actor to Hippie Leader ("Jimmy Digger"), to anti-Vietnam war protester, and underground courier for making revolution in my lifetime.

"In 1967, I came out on national television on the David Susskind Show featuring me and Abbie Hoffman. My professional acting career was pretty much killed by that one moment of truth, but it took me years to figure that out. Happenstance put me on Christopher Street as the police began to raid the Stonewall. This event changed my life forever. . . . I have remained an active political person in the building of a visible lesbian and gay culture for all our kids. . . . never wanting to be just like heterosexual society, hell-bent on transforming the world into a place that respects the individual, understands diversity, and defines humanity not by a series of checkoff points but by life practice. . . . Love is our weapon and our strength: physical, sexual, and spiritual love. My tribe still wants: to smash patriarchy that attempts to define and limit our desire, to discover our true gay and lesbian spirit and throw off the ugly, self-loathing roles defined for us (Stonewall patrons were the epitome of the oppressed nightmare . . . without identity but united in some unconscious bond of defiance and a will to live). We are still here, hidden in the '90s marketing creation of who gays and lesbians are. . . .

"The message of that spontaneous revolutionary moment in a most tacky bar has not changed. Do not be afraid to love yourself. Hate is a straight man's tool. Don't be seduced by a straight man's weapons. Hate and greed will only perpetuate the divisions that exist within our gay and lesbian society as it does to divide women and men, different colors of people, and rich and poor in the dominant society.

"Be positive and build a brave new world. And never, ever let anyone tell you not to have fun."

—Jim Fouratt, gay activist

Familiar Faces

Jim Fouratt on St. Marks Place, October 16, 1967. A street hippie, Fouratt was later a gay activist and organizer of the Gay Liberation Front as well as the Gay Activists Alliance, dedicated to securing basic rights for homosexuals.

Jean O'Leary, on the steps of City Hall, on April 30, 1974. A former nun, O'Leary was a leader of the National Gay Task Force, which sought to bring gay liberation into the mainstream of the American civil rights movement.

Jim Owles (photographed on September 29, 1982), the founding president of the Gay Activists Alliance, was the first openly gay candidate to run for political office in New York City in 1973. Owles envisioned a future in which "homosexuals would show straights that being gay means something more than the baths and bars."

16

James Baldwin, at the Village Theatre, August 25, 1967.

"A black gay person . . . is already, long before the question of sexuality comes into it, menaced and marked because he's black or she's black. The sexual question comes after the question of color; it's simply one more aspect of the danger in which all black people live." —James Baldwin

"The gay rights movement had all the more to fight back against—homophobia, racism, sexism—since it incorporated problems encountered by other, often parallel movements, like civil rights or the women's movement. Gays and lesbians have had to struggle against, among other things, ethnic, religious, sexual, and racial prejudice." —Kate Millett

Kate Millett, author of *Sexual Politics*, at the Gay Pride March, June 27, 1971.

Poet and Museum of Modern Art curator Frank O'Hara in his apartment on September 26, 1959. He was killed accidentally by a beach taxi at 3 A.M. on Fire Island in the summer of 1966. Because he wrote openly gay love poems, O'Hara was revered by the gay political movement of the 1970s.

W. H. Auden in his apartment on St. Mark's Place, January 15, 1966.

The first Stonewall anniversary march, held on June 28, 1970, was organized by the Christopher Street Liberation Day Committee, led by Foster Gunnison and Craig Rodwell.

"It is not to look to elected officials. We have to do it ourselves. We must work from the grassroots, join neighborhood and community groups in order to improve our lot. We are not their priority and should not think otherwise."
      —*David Rothenberg, Broadway publicist and political activist*

1970 March

June 28, 1970.

June 28, 1970.

June 28, 1970.

"I was playing with two little boys [when I was five years old] and they said they were going to go home to their wives. I said I was going home to my wife, too. They said 'You can't have a wife,' I said, 'Yes I can.'"
—k.d. lang

June 28, 1970.

Couple in Central Park after the march, June 28, 1970.

Years before the converted school on West 13th Street became the Lesbian and Gay Center, another abandoned public space was the vortex of gay life. A four-story building at 99 Wooster Street that was at one time a city firehouse was leased by the Gay Activists Alliance. Every Thursday evening there were general meetings, and Saturday nights brought "Liberation Dances," a cross "between Woodstock and Dante's *Inferno*," as one patron described it.

The main dance took place on the ground floor, where the general meeting space was converted into a dance hall by removing all the chairs. The basement had cans of beer in iced garbage cans. The second floor had bridge tables and a coffee nook. The third floor had a small theater and the top floor housed offices.

The GAA, according to one of its founders, Arthur Bell, was set up as an activist organization, but broadened its scope to include social and sociological aspects of gay life, which is why it opened the Firehouse. The Mattachine Society was far more conservative and thought of primarily as a "service" organization that did not conduct outside activities or run clubhouses. There were also fringe groups, like STAR (Street Transvestites Action Revolutionaries) and the Gay Revolution Party, both of which were for overthrowing and disrupting the government and other gay organizations.

The Firehouse building burned down on October 15, 1974, and the social club never reopened.

GAA Firehouse

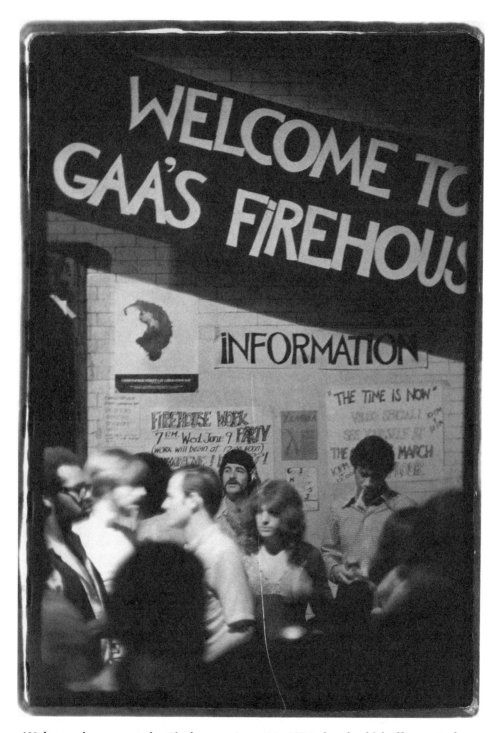

Welcome banner at the Firehouse, June 11, 1971, for the kickoff event of 1971's Gay Pride Parade.

Inside the Firehouse, June 11, 1971.

On Saturday nights, the meeting space was converted into a dance hall.

"Like racism, homophobia is in the air we breathe. 'Fag' jokes, 'lezzie' allusions, hand signals—like the pinky wetted and then moved over the eyebrow—were part of the cultural fabric of the 1950s. Limp wrists or square shoulders, a hip thrown out or a short haircut became code images for biological freaks, for people who confused others because they crossed over into territory reserved for the opposite gender. How desperate people were, and are, to defend that gender territory, perhaps the only territory some have left that they can still control."
—*Joan Nestle, cofounder, Lesbian Herstory Archives*

"The decision to come out was the end of a long struggle for me to stop conceding on the private side and having people judge me wholly on the public side. In a political time when things that were once nobody's business have now become everybody's business, it forced me to delve back on my life. People are capable of having messed up careers and wonderfully successful private lives and vice versa. It may be that you would have bad judgment that would negatively affect both. But my answer would be that during the period I was feeling weakest about my private life, people were saying nice things about my public life."
—Representative Barney Frank

"The diagnosis of homosexuality as a 'disorder' is a contributing factor to the pathology of those homosexuals who do become mentally ill. . . . Nothing is more likely to make you sick than being constantly told that you are."
—Ron Gold, National Gay and Lesbian Task Force

1971 March

Stirring up support for the march, June 21, 1971.

June 27, 1971.

June 27, 1971.

Gay Vietnam veteran, June 27, 1971.

June 27, 1971.

June 27, 1971.

June 27, 1971.

"We have got to get gay people now to do what blacks did in the '60s. Until they come out and get into political actions, we are in trouble."—Bayard Rustin, civil rights leader

"Pre-AIDS, at places like the Anvil and the Mineshaft, there was blatant, open sex, everywhere you turned. I'll never forget walking into the Mineshaft with a friend of mine from Florida. There was this man lying in a tub and getting pissed on—it's called golden showers. My friend was closeted at the time and had never seen anything like New York's sex clubs. You'd walk through these places and you'd get groped and fondled. There were guys in stirrups waiting to get anally fucked by anyone who'd come over. I used to represent a place called the Comeback Club, and one night a week there was a party called the Pubic Hair Club for Men. It was wild. But those days are virtually gone. Ever since the AIDS epidemic, while there are still sex clubs in town, most don't have the blatant stuff. The clubs that are here are packed to the gills, but there is condom distribution and a real awareness on everyone's part of the dangers of unprotected sex. Of course there are always a few renegades—people and clubs—and boy are they stupid. They're committing suicide."   *—Bruce Lynn, club promoter*

Bars and Clubs

The Ramrod, March 2, 1973, the most popular waterfront bar on West Street.

Sunday afternoon crowd outside of the Keller Bar on West Street, September 15, 1974.

The West Beach Bar, January 27, 1975; back in the early '60s, it was called the Fo'c'sle, and then became Dirty Dicks, run by Eddie "Skull" Murphy. It was the only bar in town that featured both dancing and costumes, with everything from transvestites to leather. It thrived during the '70s as the West Beach Bar, but occasionally a customer was murdered. In the '80s, it was called Badlands; today, it's a video store.

Edmund White, author of The Joy of Gay Sex, *distinctly remembers a bar he used to frequent, pre-Stonewall, called the Blue Bunny. "It was a typical joint with a bar in the front, which was sort of innocuous. Then there was a wrought-iron grille. Behind that grille there was a dance floor. And on the grille there were Christmas tree lights that would be turned on by the bartender whenever a suspicious plainclothesman would come in. When that happened, we would all instantly break apart and stop dancing."*

Eagle Tavern on the waterfront, August 31, 1971.

Carlin Jeffries performing on April 4, 1970 at a private party in an after-hours club. He became a living sculpture on a cross as a tribute to the homosexuals who died in American wars.

"Love Boys" painted on a door to an abandoned pier, March 29, 1981.

Ramrod bar, November 20, 1980, after the so-called "Ramrod Massacre." *New York Post* reporter Joe Nicholson recalls that a gunman killed four men and injured several others when he sprayed bullets into this popular waterfront bar. "I [wrote] a first-person piece on coming out and about the incident at the Ramrod [for the *Post*] . . . but the story didn't run. The editor told me that there was some concern over how Rupert Murdoch would react if it was in the paper. Maybe he didn't like gays working for him."

"Nightlife is the most superficial element of the gay community. It has always been a source of positive energy and a lot has happened with it, but a lot of people think clubs and bars are the be-all and end-all of being gay. That just isn't the case. Trends, fashions, and styles begin in the gay clubs. AIDS obviously cast a somber tone on everything and really threw people for a loop. It almost ended nightlife. But it also drew people in the gay community closer and now it is stronger than ever—with nightlife playing little part in that. It was a terrible price, but as a result the gay community has risen up to greater heights than ever." —Michael Musto, columnist, Village Voice

"I don't like where the gay rights movement is right now. It's so bourgeois, so middle class, so conformist. It's like a fundamentalist religion. You're not born again, you come out and live not according to Jesus, but to the gay standards. They've made sexuality the center of your being, which is not what we planned for."
—Dick Leitsch, Mattachine Society leader

Familiar Faces

Charles Ludlum, March 13, 1976, the director, playwright, and leading actor of the Ridiculous Theatre Company. He produced over thirty shows before his untimely death in 1987, at 44, of AIDS. His legacy consists of "Camille," "Bluebeard," "Le Bourgeois Avant-Garde," "Galas," and his final work, "How to Write a Play".

Air force sergeant Leonard Matlovich at the Gay Pride March, June 29, 1979. Matlovich did three tours of duty in Vietnam, and then was discharged for being gay. He was the first gay serviceman to file suit over his discharge, and he was successfully reinstated, collecting $160,000 in back pay. He has since died of AIDS.

Vito Russo at the Gay Pride March, June 29, 1975. He wrote *The Celluloid Closet*, a landmark exposé of Hollywood's homophobia.

Charles L. Orleb, publisher, holding the first issue of *Christopher Street*, May 26, 1976. He called it "The Gay Magazine for the Whole Family," meaning that it featured no pornography or beefcake photos.

"I don't know if its something you just find out. I guess I had thought about it as a kid. But I didn't really try it until I was in Pittsburgh, when I was twenty. The first time I didn't really like it. Then I started finding people that were nicer and more my age and more into what I was interested in." —Keith Haring, visual artist

"From his early days with the Gay Activists Alliance to cofounding Act-Up and GLAAD to his final days fighting for his own life, Vito [Russo] was always . . . at the forefront of the battle for justice. His activism inspired thousands, including me. . . . During times when it was difficult to have faith in 'leaders' it was always easy and comforting to have faith in Vito." —Lily Tomlin, actress

The end of the march, June 24, 1973.

"It is still just as hard for some people. There's a big personality quotient involved. I remember when there'd be a photographer around, if you didn't want to be in a photo, you'd go sit on the other side of the room. That rarely happens these days. We're still not home free, but things are improving daily."
—*Lee Hudson, former liaison to the lesbian and gay community under New York mayor Ed Koch*

1973 March

June 24, 1973.

Jeanne and Jules Manford march with their son Morty, along with Sarah Montgomery, June 24, 1973. According to public relations executive Ethan Geto, a year earlier Morty Manford was beaten at an annual dinner for New York's press by the fireman's union chief because he was handing out pro-gay leaflets.

"I'd always known I was gay, although I didn't know the name for it. When I was four, I had a crush on another boy. I thought all people felt that way. When I grew older, I saw my peers start to have an interest in women . . . but I didn't. I thought I was just a late bloomer. . . . But I waited and I was still interested in boys.

"Eventually I realized there was something different about me. I was fourteen or fifteen. I had heard the word 'homosexual,' knew what it meant in the dictionary, but that didn't really fit me. Somehow there was so much more involved with it than the dictionary said. There was an emotionalness on my part, and I didn't get that from the dictionary." —Sergeant Charles Cochrane, NYPD

Dr. Larry Rosen of the S & M Eulenspiegel Society, June 24, 1973.

June 24, 1973.

"I'd like to see us help gay men become more feminist. The gay women have been incredible with the AIDS crisis, and they have really come forward and contributed in any way they can. Now it's appropriate for gay men, since they have accepted our help and love and work, to work on women's issues." —Rita Mae Brown, novelist

"Street Transvestites Action Revolutionaries" (STAR) demonstrate, June 24, 1973.

Christopher Street at Sheridan Square Park, June 24, 1973.

"One of the major slogans of the gay movement is going to become the words '50 percent'—50 percent of everything. If we really believe to the core of our beings that so-called homosexuality is just as valid, just as good, just as life-giving, life-affirming as heterosexuality, then we have to believe that in the future, especially when parents and the state stop brainwashing their children, that when people have a free choice in the matter of their sexual orientation that at least 50 percent of the people are going to be gay."
—Craig Rodwell, Oscar Wilde Memorial Bookshop

"When I was growing up it was pretty common for young men, black or white, to attack gays and the victims would basically act hush hush . . . and not report anything . . . I constantly see explosive emotional violence based solely on someone's sexuality. . . . Nowadays, there's a whole new generation of attackers."
—Curtis Sliwa, Guardian Angels

1974 March

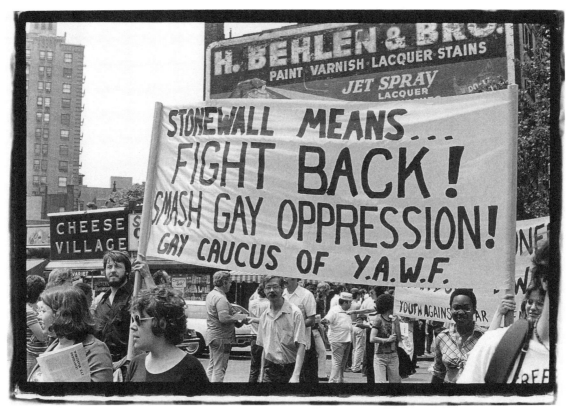

Fifth anniversary Stonewall banner carried by members of Y.A.W.F. (Youth Against War and Fascism), June 3, 1974.

"[At Stonewall], gays refused to give up their private territory of emotional expression, even when the rest of the nation was rushing headlong to drive all those who were labeled deviant from jobs, communities, and even families."
                    —*Joan Nestle, cofounder, the Lesbian Herstory Archives*

Dick Ashworth, a founding member of Parents and Friends of Lesbians and Gays
(PFLAG), marching on June 3, 1974. His son Taylor died of AIDS in 1987.

Jeanne Manford, a founding member of PFLAG, June 3, 1974.

June 3, 1974.

Gay Democrats Jim Owles and Allen Roskoff hold their banner at the march,
June 3, 1974.

Reverend Declan Daly and Sister Jeannie Gramick, Catholic leaders and members of Dignity, supporters of gay rights, June 3, 1974.

"The media is instrumental in determining people's social attitudes toward minority groups, especially gays and lesbians, who are often invisible in the mainstream press. . . . Ninety-five percent of the time we encounter defamation it is based on pure ignorance." —*Donald Suggs, GLAAD (Gay and Lesbian Alliance Against Defamation)*

"[LAMBDA's] goal was to be as forceful and important as the NAACP legal defense fund or the NOW legal defense fund were to those movements. I think we did pretty well."
—*Tom Stoddard, founder LAMBDA*

"I came out in 1971 in the pages of New York *magazine. Looking back, it did not help my career. In a large majority of American cities coverage of gays and gay issues is minimal to nonexistent. So except for a few outlets, gay journalists are not going to come out for fear of losing their jobs, or worse."* —*Doug Ireland, journalist*

"Blacks cover other blacks, women cover other women. If you're a good reporter, your color, gender, or sexuality should not figure into your work. I defy you or anyone else to show me even one example where my personal orientation had any influence whatsoever on my work."
—**New York Times** *reporter Jeffrey Schmalz, who died of AIDS in 1993*

1975 March

June 29, 1975.

"We live in a society where differences in race, religion, culture, gender, physical ability, and sexual orientation are too often met with hostile and brutal acts. This must stop. . . . The first step toward stopping it is the enactment of specific legislation declaring it to be unacceptable, illegal, a punishable crime."
—former New York mayor David Dinkins

June 29, 1975.

June 29, 1975.

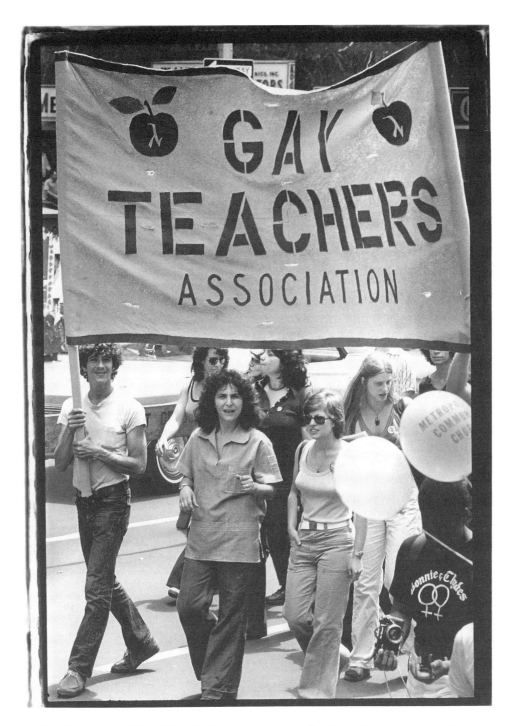

Gay Teachers; Meryl C. Friedman, the organization's head, is in center, June 29, 1975.

"At first, I thought the gay liberation movement would turn the Village into a ghetto. To me, everything was much sexier before the riots, the clandestine aspect of everything excited me. It was much sexier to sneak around, don't you think? I liked it before everyone wore mustaches and combat boots and started going to bed with their own lookalikes. That isn't any fun. When everyone and everything came out it all became so indiscriminate, with people doing people in the back rooms of bars. Unfortunately, too many people wound up with AIDS from that.

"But don't misunderstand me. It was a necessary movement nevertheless. I myself was picked up by detectives twice that I remember in the '50s and wound up in the Tombs. That was a horrifying and humiliating experience. It happened to thousands of us, I'd imagine. There had to be a reaction to that and it was the riots and the whole movement.

"The best part is the great political power that homosexuals have amassed since then. Twenty-five years ago, we were barely a blip. Nobody recognized that there was a gay voting bloc. Now, the candidates all come a courtin' to Christopher Street. It's amazing how things have changed."

—Taylor Mead, poet and actor

June 29, 1975.

June 29, 1975.

Members of the Gay Activists Alliance of New Jersey, June 29, 1975.

June 29, 1975.

John Noble and Bishop Robert Clement, leaders of the world's first gay church, The Church of the Beloved Disciple, June 29, 1975.

"I have the best job in American Judaism. Friends warned me about taking the job. They feared I was committing career suicide. But Judaism has taught me that it's important to take risks. I think CBST represents much of what is best about American Judaism . . . even if America doesn't know it yet."
    —Rabbi Sharon Kleinbaum, Congregation Beth Simchat Torah (a gay synagogue)

June 29, 1975.

Cross-dressing is so far in, it's almost become passé. When writer Jay McInerney and several other heterosexual men appeared in drag at the fortieth anniversary party for *Paris Review* magazine in 1993, there were groans all around.

While Ru Paul, the drag queen who has topped the record charts in 1992, was a shock to America's system, the phenomenon of cross-dressing has been well represented in film and on stage for decades. Modern-day examples include Tony Curtis and Jack Lemmon in *Some Like it Hot*, Dustin Hoffman in *Tootsie*, Julie Andrews in *Victor/Victoria*, and Robin Williams in *Mrs. Doubtfire*. Phil Donahue made a splash when he appeared in drag on one of his shows about cross-dressing. In the armed forces and all-male colleges, where there often were no women available to play female roles, men have a long history of cross-dressing in performance; Princeton University's famous Triangle Club all-male kickline being but one notable example.

The men who dress as women for personal expression view their femme creation as a means of expressing the kinder, gentler, more emotional aspect of their personalities. A transformation really does take place. There is electrolysis, wigs, makeup, nail tips, and lingerie. Their reasons for gender bending are as varied as their personal backgrounds. Some men had mothers who wanted daughters, so they dressed them as girls from birth; others grew up as the only male in an all-female household; and still others feel they were meant to live as women. Some simply enjoy the camp aspect of playing a woman's role. Others are trying to emphasize a gender-neutral look; Madonna dresses both as a campy Marilyn Monroe, a man in a business suit, a peep-show dancer, and various other male/female hybrids in her videos, while Charles Ludlum appeared both as men and women in various roles in his famous productions at the Ridiculous Theatre Company.

"I was talking to John Waters the other day. He told me that if Divine was alive, he'd be jealous of all the attention Ru Paul is getting these days. Ru does get a lot of attention, but it's still light-years before Ru or anyone else like him gets their own sitcom, for example. New York and a few other places are enlightened. Much of the rest of the world isn't. The gay movement has come a long way over the last twenty-five years, but there's still a long way to go. Almost every day there is another amazing breakthrough. But since we started pretty late, there's still a long way to go."
—*Michael Musto, columnist,* Village Voice

Cross-dressers

Divine (aka Harris G. Milstead), photographed in his New York penthouse, February 28, 1980. Divine was discovered by filmmaker John Waters, who featured him in many of his films, including *Female Trouble, Pink Flamingos*, and *Hairspray*. He later died of AIDS.

The All-American Camp Beauty Pageant held at New York's Town Hall, February 20, 1967. Miss Philadelphia won first place. The judges included Terry Southern, Larry Rivers, Rona Jaffe, Jim Dine, Baby Jane Holzer, Paul Krassner, and Andy Warhol.

"I think the largest problem facing the gay and lesbian community is the same as the largest problem facing the City of New York—crime and unsafe conditions on the streets. This reflects itself in gays and lesbians being attacked because they're gay or lesbian. I would say that is the first problem facing the gay and lesbian community both as part of the general population of the city and as gays and lesbians."
—New York mayor Rudolph Giuliani

Mr. Gina from Costa Rica wearing a Henri Lissaver designer dress at a Mattachine Society ball, October 27, 1967.

Spacemen at a Mattachine Society ball, October 27, 1967, held at the famous, very seedy Hotel Diplomat on West 44th Street.

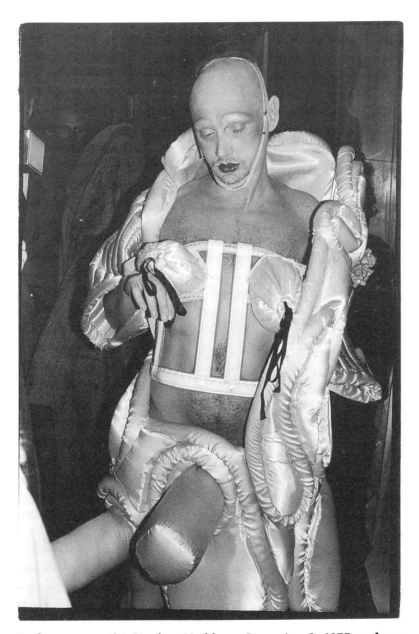

Performance artist Stephen Varble on December 2, 1975 performing at the Rizzoli Bookstore. His costume depicts a transsexual car-crash victim with protruding, silk-covered penis and breasts.

Opera star Eleanor Steber, photographed on October 1, 1973, was one of the many celebrities who performed at the Continental Baths during its peak years. The baths were closed down a year later.

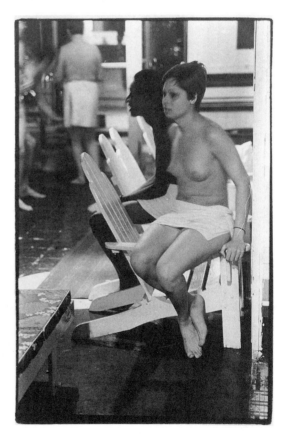

Transsexual-in-progress at the Continental Baths, December 19, 1973.

The Cockettes, an acting troupe from San Francisco, photographed on October 30, 1971 during their New York production of *Tinsel Tarts in a Hot Coma*, a satire of 1930s musical comedies.

Along with soup cans, Marilyn lithographs, excruciatingly dull twenty-four-hour black and white movies, and *Interview* magazine, Andy Warhol's Factory turned out people. Warhol was called Pop, and his product was the Kids: Viva, Candy Darling, Ultra Violet, Baby Jane Holzer, and Edie Sedgwick. They all spent time on the Factory's production line, located in its glory days at Union Square on Broadway and 17th Street. Together, Warhol and his glamorous, wacky, and unusual mix of offspring epitomize for many the 1960s. Sexuality, too, was one thing many Factory denizens were famous for. Candy Darling, for example, began life as James Slattery from Long Island. Jackie Curtis was as likely to show up as a man or as a woman. Holly Woodlawn was in fact a Stonewall patron. "I had my own gang to run with except that we were a bunch of mad queens who invaded the Stonewall every night and had a ball," she wrote in her memoirs, *Low Life in High Heels*.

The Factory was the epicenter of Warhol. And whatever else one says about him, he possessed an infallible Midas touch. Everything he did or touched, and precisely because he touched it, either turned to gold or became a matter of celebrity. "The one thing that unites us all at the Factory is our urgent, over-whelming need to be noticed," said Ultra Violet.

Warhol and Friends

Candy Darling and Tom Eyen, May 8, 1972, at the OBIE awards. Candy played the lead in Eyen's *Give My Regards to Off-Off Broadway*.

Liz Eden and Littlejohn Wojtowicz, March 2, 1979. They were the subjects of the black comedy film *Dog Day Afternoon*, starring Al Pacino. Pacino portrayed Littlejohn, who robbed a bank so he could pay for his boyfriend's sex-change operation.

Jackie Curtis, December 7, 1970, a Warhol "superstar."

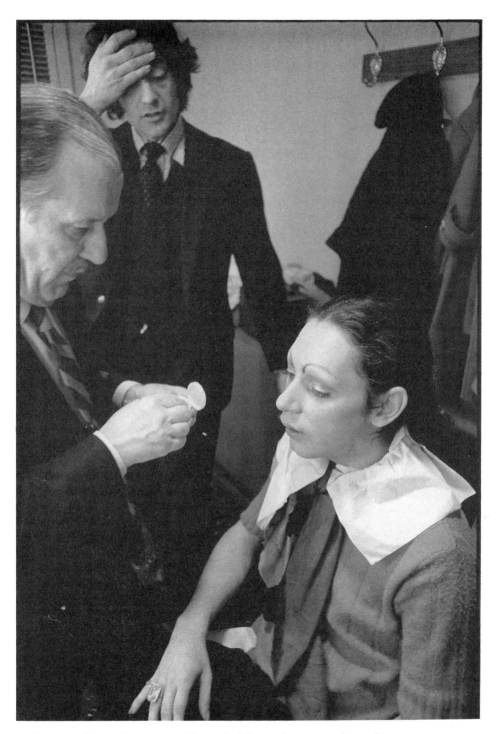

Holly Woodlawn (born Harold Danhakl) putting on makeup for an appearance on the *David Susskind* show, December 7, 1970. He/she was the star of Andy Warhol's *Trash*.

Candy Darling (born James Slattery), December 7, 1970, was one of the best female impersonators in the theater. She later died of cancer.

Robert Mapplethorpe, photographer, in his Bond Street studio, December 22, 1979. Mapplethorpe's estate has donated $1 million to establish a residence for AIDS patients at the Beth Israel Medical Center in New York.

On Robert Mapplethorpe: "Art does not set out to be acceptable. It often deals with the extremes of the human condition. It is not to be expected that . . . everyone is going to be happy with it. Particularly museum art, which people are free to come to see, or not see. Many museums show things that are not palatable to everybody. It is really important to understand that art often bites, it can really touch raw nerves. If it were popularly accepted, art would not need all the help that it gets. There's got to be a real distinction made between art and entertainment."
—Stephen Weil, deputy director, Hirschhorn Museum, Washington, D.C.

Familiar Faces

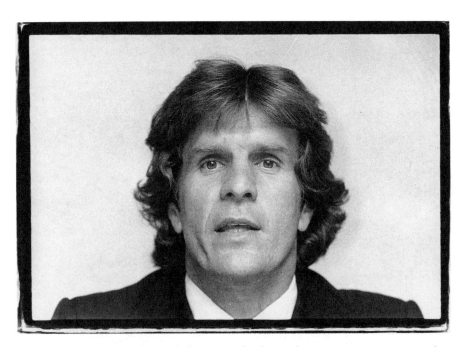

Ex-NFL player David Kopay, photographed March 4, 1977, at a press conference announcing he was gay. He was the first professional athlete to do so. After his retirement, he hoped to work as an athletics coach: "No one would hire me. . . . They didn't think I could fill the role of coach as guardians of the morals of the young students."

Liberace, March 27, 1985: "I find it equally natural to speak of 'Mr. Showmanship' Liberace as if he were another person. The man behind the music, the glamour, the glitz . . . is another Liberace."

Truman Capote (born Truman Strekfus Persona) photographed at a book-signing party, March 21, 1978.

"I never had any problem about being homosexual. I mean, look at me. I was always right out there. The other kids liked me for that. I was really quite popular. I was amusing and I was pretty. I didn't look like anybody else and I wasn't like anybody else." —Truman Capote, author

Tennessee Williams (b. Thomas Lanier Williams) photographed in his West 43rd Street apartment, January 3, 1980.

"If you're writing about men, you're writing about men. And if you're writing about women, write about women. Tennessee Williams knew the difference as well as I do." —Edward Albee, playwright

Gay Men's Chorus, September 27, 1982. West Coast counterparts include the Lesbian/Gay Chorus of San Francisco; the Bay Area Lesbian Choral Ensemble; and the San Francisco Men's Chorus.

"The Gay Men's Chorus—150 voices strong—has for a dozen years brought lumps to our throats and tears to our eyes with songs of love, pain and courage; smiles to our lips with the lighter numbers; and pride and gladness to our hearts with their sincerity, dedication, and lyricism." —Bruce-Michael Gelbert, music critic, New York Native

Historian Jonathan Katz, August 2, 1980, in his office. He is the author of *Gay American History* and *The Gay and Lesbian Almanac*.

Halston at Studio 54, September 4, 1979.

Jill Johnston, author of *Lesbian Nation*, at the Gay Pride March, June 27, 1971.

June 27, 1982.

1982 March

June 27, 1982.

June 27, 1982.

"My sexuality has definitely cost me a lot of money. The bottom line is that Madison Avenue is run by white, male yuppies. My forthrightness and sexual preference long ago scared away advertisers. But I'd rather have it like this than pretend to be Miss Heterosexual America. I'd rather be who I am and make less. After all, I've made more than my share of money playing tennis." —Martina Navratilova, tennis champion

"For almost twenty years, the movement has been almost entirely reactive, careening from event to event—a court victory here, an electoral loss there. Now we need to unify as never before, working across organizational lines and consolidating resources to develop a national plan of action—that gay agenda we've been accused of promoting." —Torie Olson, past director, Los Angeles Gay and Lesbian Community Services Center

June 27, 1982.

Since 1984, the old P.S. 6 school building on Manhattan's West 13th Street has been home to the Lesbian and Gay Community Services Center, delivering social, cultural, and medical services to homosexuals and others. Approximately four hundred groups rent space for meetings and other events, and several organizations are headquartered there, including the Coalition for Lesbian and Gay Rights, SAGE (Senior Action in a Gay Environment), Center Kids, Lesbian Switchboard, the Pat Parker and Vito Russo Library, Youth Enrichment Services, and the Community Health Project. Act-Up, Queer Nation, and GLAAD all had their first meetings in the space. The National Museum of Lesbian and Gay History and Archive was launched there in 1989 to produce exhibitions and provide resources for researchers.

The center has played a large part in the transformation of the gay-rights movement. "Once our enemies viewed us as weak and ineffectual. Now they characterize us as members of a rich and powerful elite, a special interest conspiracy threatening to dominate the government and media," proclaimed Richard Burns, the center's director, on its tenth anniversary. "We need an organized, activist, broad-based community to push our agenda regardless of the prevailing political climate. That's why the center is vital to our struggle. It builds community in so many different ways. The center, by its very being, promotes community organizing. Many of the groups that use the center would not exist without us."

Lesbian and Gay Community Services Center

Annual garden party at the Lesbian and Gay Community Services Center,
June 24, 1991.

An enthusiastic crowd at the center shouts approval during a rally for then
mayoral candidate David Dinkins on November 2, 1989.

Ruth Messinger, Manhattan Borough President, at the community center, November 2, 1989. Her daughter Miriam came out while a student at Harvard. With Messinger are (l to r): Diane D'Allessandro, Tony Whitfield, Leslie Cagan, and Nancy Wackstein.

Campaigning at the center, November 2, 1989, Dinkins promises to support the Domestic Partnership and Gay Rights Bill. Standing with him are (l to r) Marjorie Hill, Tom Duane, Barbara Turk, and David Kirby.

June 25, 1989.

1989 March

June 25, 1989.

June 25, 1989.

June 25, 1989.

June 25, 1989.

Latino Lesbians (The Good Friends) lead off the march from Columbus Circle, June 30, 1991.

"If Mayor Rudy Giuliani empowers any gay people at all it will be gay people whose careers are more important to them than gay politics . . . I think we're going to see gay Republicans emerge in the city for the first time, which is a good thing."
—*Richard Goldstein, executive editor, Village Voice*

1991 March

June 30, 1991.

"I don't make fun of myself and I steer away from self-deprecating humor. I search for universal themes, although I do perform specifically lesbian material."
—Kate Clinton, lesbian comic

June 30, 1991.

June 30, 1991.

Curbs along the march route were lined with supporters, June 30, 1991.

"In March 1990, Tom Blewitt, Michelangelo Signoreli, Karl Soehnlein, and myself, all longtime members of Act-Up, got together. It was about the time when Andy Rooney made some cracks about gays to the Advocate. We wanted to do something, but we realized that Act-Up was designed to deal with AIDS issues, not this or other antigay incidents. We decided to explore the possibility of doing something more about gay and lesbian issues.

"At our first meeting, sixty people showed up. We were stunned. At our second meeting, eighty-five people showed up. Soon after that someone planted a crude pipe bomb at Uncle Charlie's bar. I think it was on a Friday night. The four of us heard about it Saturday morning. We called everyone we knew. That Saturday night we had twelve hundred people on the street to protest antigay and lesbian violence.

"At the beginning of the day we didn't have a name. Then I remembered a rally protesting the FDA down in Maryland a few years earlier by an ad hoc protest group called Queer Nation. I thought it was funny and provocative. So I took the bullhorn and announced that the rally had been sponsored by Queer Nation. The New York Times reported on it the next day and referred to Queer Nation. The name stuck.

"The next really big action drew international press. It was in April and called the first 'queers bash back' demonstration. We marched from the West Village to the East Village and back to the piers. For the first time you saw gays and lesbians fighting back, running after bottle throwers and confronting them. We had about fifteen hundred people that day.

"We've also started a queer shopping network where we have groups travel to nearby malls and hand out leaflets about safe sex. On 'Nights Out,' we go to straight bars, like the old Fluties at South Street Seaport or McSorley's Old Ale House, and try to confront people's stereotypes.

"It really made some of them think.

"There are now about fifty Queer Nation chapters and it is encouraging that many of them are on college campuses. Kids today can be unapologetically gay and they are really affecting pop culture and the future."

—Alan Klein, cofounder, Queer Nation

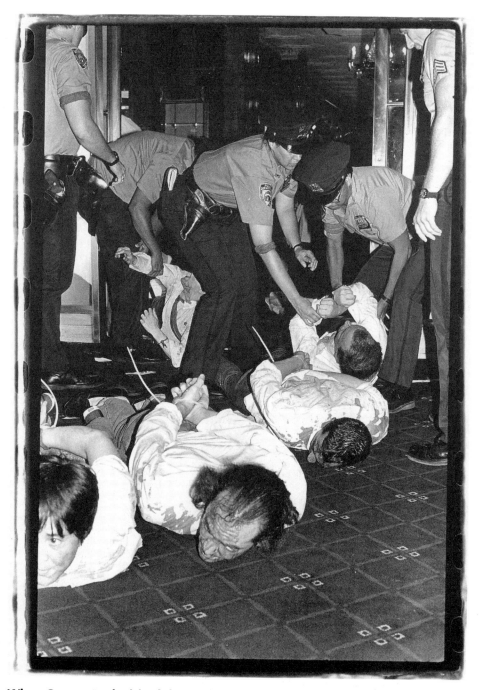

When George Bush visited the Waldorf-Astoria Hotel on August 24, 1990, Act-Up called attention to the AIDS disaster by demonstrating in the hotel lobby.

Act-Up demonstrating at City Hall for AIDS housing and counseling, drug-treatment facilities, and children's centers, March 28, 1989.

Act-Up poster announces frequency of AIDS deaths, March 28, 1989.

Gay Urban Truth Squad of Dallas, at the Democratic National Convention, July 17, 1988 in Atlanta. The Nazis made homosexuals wear inverted pink triangles as identification, just as Jews were forced to wear yellow Stars of David. In the 1970s, gay activists adopted the pink triangle (seen in the center of the banner) as a way of remembering that gays were one of the many minorities persecuted by the Nazis.

Act-Up demonstrators stopping traffic at the Brooklyn Bridge to create public awareness for the AIDS crisis, March 28, 1989.

Act-Up of Los Angeles, demonstrating at the Democratic National Convention, New York City, July 15, 1992.

Larry Kramer, playwright and activist, photographed on Union Square at a rally to save the National Endowment for the Arts, May 15, 1990. Kramer was among the founders of Gay Men's Health Crisis and Act-Up and the author of *The Normal Heart*.

"In 1970, the late Marty Robinson of the Political Action Committee of the Gay Activists Alliance (GAA) proposed that the group work for an amendment to New York City's human rights law that would ban discrimination against lesbians and gay men. The movement's emphasis in those heady, combative days was on getting rid of sodomy laws (not accomplished until the state court threw them out in 1980), ending police harassment and entrapment, and expanding gay consciousness, liberation, and social life.

"Even at a time when movements for the civil rights of African-Americans and women were at their height, it was radical to suggest that gay people should receive equal treatment. GAA even had trouble getting liberal city council members from Manhattan to sign on as co-sponsors of the legislation. But several years of relentless militant activism led by the late Jimmy Owles and Morty Manford, among others, paid off in 1974 when the sexual orientation bill was voted out of the General Welfare Committee 7-1. No bill in the city's history had ever been approved by committee and lost on the floor of the full council. Thanks to a vicious campaign led by the Roman Catholic Archdiocese of New York, this one was rejected.

"The church had a stooge in Thomas Cuite, the council majority leader, who ruled with an iron hand. Cuite promised Cardinal Cooke that the bill would not see the light of day, and he succeeded in keeping that pledge despite the support of all city officials, the governor, the major newspapers, and public opinion polls.

"The Coalition for Lesbian and Gay Rights brought gay and mainstream groups together to work for passage. The Gay Rights Bill was a subject before city council members twenty-eight times beginning January 6, 1971, but was always defeated. Even these losses, however, produced memorable moments. Bob Livingston, the city's first openly gay Human Rights Commissioner, on the verge of death in 1981, struggled to the podium at the public hearing to promise, 'We will be back again and again and again.' Sergeant Charles Cochrane, NYPD, also testified in 1981, saying, 'I am proud to be a police officer. And I am equally proud to be gay'. Betty Santoro, of Lesbian Feminist Liberation (LFL), the lead testifier in 1983, asked, 'Do we have to stand here bleeding before you to convince you that we have suffered enough to deserve our rights?' David Rothenberg in 1981 spoke of a horrific incident the year before when four gay men were gunned down in the Village outside the Ramrod Bar by a crazed anti-gay bigot.

"But in 1986—well into the reign of Ronald Reagan and the dispiriting AIDS crisis— all those years of bitter struggle paid off. With the emergence of a gay political action committee (FAIRPAC) and gay political clubs in every borough, a new council had been elected with a bare majority committed to vote for the bill. LAMBDA Legal Defense's Tom Stoddard drafted a new version of the bill, clarifying its intent without watering it down. The new Catholic archbishop, John O'Connor, upheld his group's tradition of bigoted opposition, but he was more than counterbalanced by the common decency of religious leaders such as Episcopal bishop Paul Moore, Rabbi Balfour Brickner, and, in his own church, Sister Jeannine Gramick, Reverend Bernard Lynch, and the members of Dignity.

"We took nothing for granted. Thousands of letters supporting the Gay Rights Bill were piled on council members' desks. Gay leaders as diverse as Allen Roskoff and Jim Levin worked together in common cause. Political consultant Ethan Geto worked the inside while lesbian leader Eleanor Cooper organized the grassroots. The Gay and

Politics

Lesbian Alliance Against Defamation emerged to help with street activism. On March 11, the bill passed committee 5-1. And on March 20, 1986, after fifteen years of struggle, the bill in full council passed by a 21-14 vote, with Council Member Ruth Messinger casting the deciding vote.

"But the United States Supreme Court dealt us a setback almost immediately, in June, 1986, when it ruled 5-4 in the infamous Bowers v. Hardwick decision that state laws prohibiting consensual sex between members of the same sex were constitutional, reminding us that we have a long way to go before enjoying equal justice in the land of the free.

"In 1971, New York City was the first to propose protecting civil rights on the basis of sexual orientation. When the Gay Rights Bill passed in 1986, many jurisdictions had codified gay rights, and several, including Dade County, Houston, and Wichita, had repealed them through referenda. Today, eight states—Wisconsin, Vermont, California, Massachusetts, Hawaii, Connecticut, New Jersey, and Minnesota—but not New York—protect gay rights, as do hundreds of cities and counties. These laws are the prime target in the religious right wing's nation-wide effort to seize political power by attacking 'special rights for homosexuals'. We always knew we were special. We have never wanted anything more from the government, however, than equal treatment under the law.

"Many of the visionaries who conceived of a 'gay rights law' and worked for its passage here in New York City are gone—burned out, retired, or dead from AIDS or other causes. They can rest in peace knowing that the revolution they started, while far from over, has spawned a generation that is growing up protected by the law and much freer to help everyone understand what gay liberation is all about."

—Andy Humm, Cable News Network

Sergeant Charles Cochrane, a New York City cop for fourteen years, appeared on November 20, 1981 before the City Council to testify in support of the Gay Rights Bill.

Jean O'Leary and Lieutenant Governor Mary Ann Krupsak at City Hall supporting the Gay Rights Bill, September 11, 1975.

Bill Bahlman and playwright Harvey Fierstein (*Torch Song Trilogy*) at a City Council hearing for the Gay Rights Bill, March 11, 1986.

Mayor Edward I. Koch speaking at the City Council hearing in favor of the Gay Rights Bill, March 11, 1986. Seated (l to r): Joyce Hunter, David Gilbert, Eleanor Cooper, Allen Roskoff, Andy Humm.

Arthur Bell, founding member of Gay Activists Alliance and newspaper columnist for the *Village Voice*, along with *Voice* media critic Doug Ireland, September 11, 1975.

Thomas K. Duane at City Hall, January 8, 1992. Duane is the first openly gay, HIV positive person to be elected to New York's City Council. He serves on the land use, parks, recreation, and cultural affairs committees.

Deborah Glick, New York State Assembly Member, April 9, 1991. The first openly gay state legislator, she was reelected in 1992 with a 98 percent victory over her opponent.

"A lot of people were really surprised to see that I am a regular person, despite my sexual orientation. . . . Until my colleagues met me, I don't think they knew exactly what to expect. To some people, I will always be 'the lesbian.' You know, now that I think about it, I've really had more trouble here being a woman than a lesbian. There's a lot more sexism than homophobia in the hallowed halls of the legislature." —Deborah Glick

"No modern community, other than in wartime, has had to confront a crisis such as the one the gay community has faced over the last decade. The calamity of AIDS has befallen mankind at a time when the gay community was still young, carefree, and not at all organized to deal with a massive health emergency; and, worse, at a time when established institutions were steeped in homophobia and bigotry and when the resources needed to inform, educate, and care for the ill and the poor in the gay community were repeatedly denied. . . . Remarkably, despite the fact that the gay and lesbian community carried the heaviest burden of misery and disease caused by HIV/AIDS . . . gays and lesbians came together in an extraordinary show of compassion and solidarity in response to AIDS. . . . It is the gay community's efforts that first demonstrated that the spread of HIV/AIDS could be virtually stopped through peer-led educational programs and it is the gay and lesbian community who demonstrated how best to care for those afflicted through the hundreds of community-based support and service organizations it founded and financed."

—*Dr. Mathilde Krim, co-founder and chair of American Foundation for AIDS Research (AmFAR)*

People With Aids at the Gay Rights March, June 25, 1989

"We are leading the fight to educate the public and prevent the spread of the virus—because, until we have a cure, prevention is the only way to avert the massive human, social, and economic costs of AIDS." —*Dr. Mervyn F. Silverman, president of AMFAR*

Early London subway posters, mid-'80s.

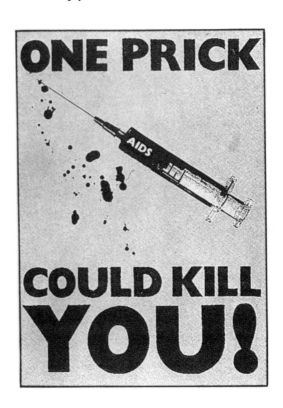

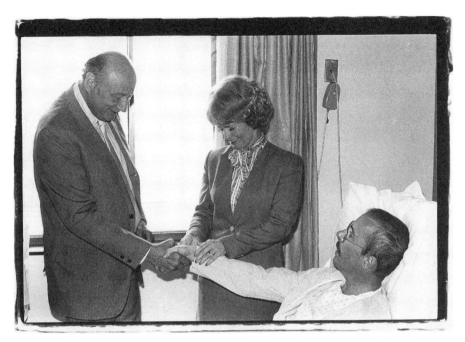

U.S. Health Secretary Margaret M. Heckler and Mayor Koch visit Peter Justice at Cabrini Medical Center, August 24, 1983. The center is a fifty-two bed unit dedicated to treating HIV patients.

Anti-Koch demonstrators, March 28, 1989.

Volunteer Alice Carey from the Gay Men's Health Center handed out condoms to commuters at the World Trade Center, November 26, 1991, until security guards escorted her from the premises.

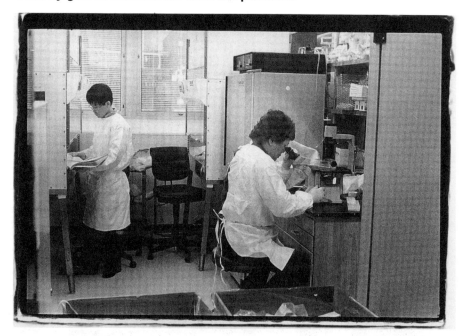

Aaron Diamond AIDS Research Center, April 16, 1991. It is one of the largest scientific facilities created to perform AIDS research, under the direction of Dr. David D. Ho, with fifty scientists and state-of-the-art research labs.

June 25, 1989.

June 30, 1991.

Brad Davis, March 11, 1980. Davis was the French sailor in "Querelle" who goes ashore in the port of Brest to find sex in a brothel, only to discover his own homosexuality. He was in the TV drama "The Normal Heart," as well as the film "Midnight Express."

"I have the same vantage on the Stonewall riots as I do on the Boston Tea Party. They were both blows for freedom. Obviously, Stonewall was the beginning of gay people emerging into society as a positive force. But, I'd have to say it has not affected the entertainment industry even one little bit. What major leading men these days are saying that they are gay? Sure, [producer] David Geffen is liberated, but he can afford to be. . . . I know there are some well-known leading men and women in the field today who are gay but have not publicly said so. It is a business decision as much as anything else. If they did, they'd be throwing in the towel for future prime acting roles."
—Liz Smith, gossip columnist

Familiar Faces

Rock Hudson, December 16, 1980.

Elizabeth Taylor, March 6, 1978. Rock Hudson's death, along with the diagnosis of her daughter-in-law, Aileen Getty, with AIDS, galvanized Taylor into becoming one of the leading fund-raisers for AIDS research, as well as a spokesperson for people with the disease.

Dick Leitsch, in Sheridan Square Park, August 21, 1969.

Craig Rodwell, October 14, 1969, at the Oscar Wilde Memorial Bookshop, then located at 291 Mercer Street. It is one of the nation's leading stores for serious literature on gay and lesbian issues.

Dr. Mathilde Krim, AIDS researcher.

"I'm personally rather shy and retiring, and I would prefer to be ensconced in a lab. This isn't necessarily the role I'd choose to play. But I use my contacts because I do feel that it's my duty."
                    —*Dr. Mathilde Krim, AmFAR*

Virginia Apuzzo, former executive director, National Gay Task Force, at an awards ceremony in New York City Controller Liz Holzman's office, June 26, 1991.

Essayist, poet, and novelist Jewelle Gomez and Herstory archivist Joan Nestle, at an awards ceremony in Liz Holzman's office, June 26, 1991.

"There is a tremendous amount of lesbian baiting in the military. Any straight man who propositions a woman and she's not interested, well, it can't be because he's not attractive. So it must be because she's a lesbian. It's used as a threat all the time."
—Colonel Margarethe Cammermeyer, discharged nurse, Army National Guard

David Mixner, Clinton administration advisor, April 25, 1993.

Margarethe Cammermeyer, photographed April 25, 1993, was the chief nurse of the Washington, D.C. National Guard before being discharged for being a lesbian. A bronze star and Meritorious Service medal winner in Vietnam, she was subject to a security clearance in 1989 when she was being considered for Chief Nurse of the National Guard. Married and the mother of four sons, she admitted that she was now a lesbian, and was "separated" from her post and rank.

Before 1942, there was no specific ordinance, rule, or law barring homosexuals from serving in the U.S. military. In that year, military psychiatrists warned of the "psychopathic personality disorders" that make gays unfit to serve. During the repressive era that followed, discharges for homosexuality soared. According to the federal General Accounting Office, chasing suspected homosexuals out of the military cost the Pentagon about $27 million per year. That does not include the human cost of ruined careers and disrupted lives. Gay rights activists have been fighting the Pentagon for decades, working to change their minds that homosexuality is not a threat to discipline in the ranks and national security.

The issue of gays in the military returned to the front pages in October 1991 when candidate Bill Clinton promised he'd do for gays what Harry Truman had done for blacks in the service: eliminate the military's discriminatory policies by executive order. Since then, several celebrated cases have crystallized the issue. Keith Meinhold came out on national television (on ABC's *World News Tonight*) in May 1993, and was discharged in August. In November, a court order sent him back to his Mountain View, CA naval base. "I don't see myself as a hero," he said, "But it is important to me to do this right. I will be a test case, and hopefully I won't make any mistakes that will jeopardize my position or the position of other gays and lesbians."

To date, the Pentagon has shelved its "don't ask, don't tell" policy, due to a federal district court order allowing gay service members to serve openly without fear of punishment; the government is appealing this decision. Gay rights leaders applaud the action, but urge people to use caution in disclosing their true sexuality, lest the disclosure be used against them if the injunction is lifted by a higher court.

Gays in the Military

Petty officer Keith Meinhold, seen here at the March on Washington, April 25, 1993, was expelled from the Navy after announcing he was gay. Later, he won a court decision that led to his reinstatement.

Allen Ginsberg and Peter Orlovsky in their East Village apartment, November 1, 1964.

"In the '40s the Bomb dropped. In the '40s the entire planet was threatened biologically. In the '40s there was a recovery from a total breakdown of all morality in the concentration camps. For those of us who were homosexual, it was the realization of, what are we being intimidated by a bunch of jerks who don't know anything about life? Who were they to tell us what to feel and how we're supposed to behave?" —Allen Ginsberg

Domestic Partners

Artist Don Bachardy and Christopher Isherwood, March 28, 1979; they lived together as an openly gay couple for thirty-three years.

"The idea of declaring your homosexuality seems so simple. I regret I didn't do it earlier in one way or another and I think perhaps I should have. But I never felt that I was concealing it, as far as my own life and my own relations with other people were concerned. In the first place, over a great period of my life I lived in a domestic relationship with some other man, and we've always gone around everywhere together, and there's never been any question about that, so there's never been any question of covering up in any sort of way. That makes a difference." —Christopher Isherwood

Jill Johnston and Ingrid Nyeboe, October 27, 1993.

Jill Johnston and Ingrid Nyeboe have been a couple since December 1980. They were married in Denmark under a domestic-partnership law in June 1993, and marked the event with a gathering in New York City in October. Johnston said, "It's really a natural thing to do and I couldn't be happier. We've been together thirteen years. [The Danish domestic-partnership law] was the first one like it in the world. It confers benefits on married partners and makes me eligible for health insurance there if I was to have a serious medical problem. I may be the first foreigner—one partner must be Danish—to marry under the new law. Between four hundred and five hundred couples have married in Denmark, more male couples than female. On April 1, 1993, Norway passed the same law and I've read that Sweden is next."

Applying for domestic partnership status, March 1, 1993. L to r: Gary Sechen, Wynn Miller, Fredda Rubin, Katia Netto.

The City of New York
AFFIDAVIT OF DOMESTIC PARTNERSHIP

Affidavit of Domestic Partnership, City of New York.

Robert Levy and David Schutte register as domestic partners, March 1, 1993.

There is a long tradition of public demonstrations in Washington, D.C. to protest important issues of the day. In our century, we have seen World War I veterans march for their bonuses, farmers during the Depression demanding more federal support, and of course, the first great march on Washington for civil rights in 1963, led by Dr. Martin Luther King, Jr., followed by rallies for peace inspired by the Vietnam War. In 1993, an estimated one million gays, lesbians, and their supporters convened in the capital city to march for their rights.

For one weekend, the entire city was transformed into a celebration of sexuality. With panache and swagger, in leather and cashmere, in song and prayer, people came from around the world to march for their rights. And, of course, to have fun; "We're here, we're queer, so drink beer" was a common rallying cry.

But the premise of the march was serious. The weekend's platform included support for a lesbian, gay, bisexual, and transgender civil rights bill, massive increase in AIDS funding, antidiscrimination legislation, reproductive freedom, and the inclusion of nontraditional lifestyles in school curricula.

The weekend also featured a display of the AIDS quilt. Six months earlier, the full, fifteen-acre, twenty-one-thousand-panel quilt was laid out around the Washington Monument, spreading out like a mammoth bouquet in honor of those who have died of AIDS. Panels for individuals ranging from Peter Allen, Rock Hudson, and Ryan White to everyday people were represented. The quilt is a living memorial to the tragic toll that AIDS has taken on the American community, a silent but very powerful call to further action in the war against AIDS.

Washington, D.C.

Antiwar march on Constitution Avenue during the Nixon inauguration included gay pride protesters, January 20, 1973.

April 25, 1993 march; in the front line marched New York City Public Advocate Mark Green and Congressman Jerrold Nadler.

"Too many people in this country are still saying, 'This is somebody else's problem, in somebody else's city, not mine.' Older gay men are changing their patterns of behavior, but younger gay men are still engaging in . . . sexual behavior that [is] risky."
—Kristine Gebbie, National AIDS Czar

Washington Monument with the NAMES Project AIDS Memorial Quilt, October 10, 1992.

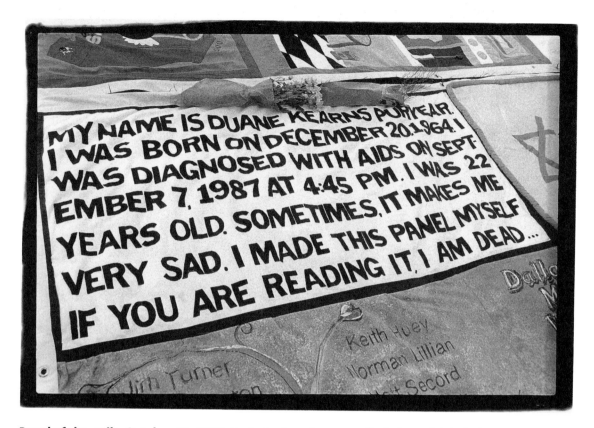

Panel of the quilt, October 10, 1992. Each cluster of sewn quilts is boxed, labeled, and spread out within set guide lines.

"Like Dr. Martin Luther King, who marched this same route some thirty years ago, we, too, are people with a dream."
—*Reverend Donald Eastman*

October 10, 1992. The names on the quilts run a broad spectrum of society: Michael Bennett, Perry Ellis, Robert Mapplethorpe, Keith Haring, Wayland Flowers, Halston, Liberace, Sylvester, Charles Ludlum, and Roy Cohn.

October 10, 1992.

"I know I paid a terrible political price for saying that the time had come to end the categorical ban on gays and lesbians serving in our military. . . . If somebody is willing to die for their country, should they have the right to do it? I think the answer is yes."
—President Bill Clinton

Act-Up demonstration outside of the White House, April 25, 1993; President Clinton is seen as Pinocchio.

Larry Kramer, playwright and activist, addressing a meeting of New York state doctors and health-care professionals: "I hate people like you. People who think they're so noble because you think you're taking care of the world and that makes you saints. You're all murderers. The best thing that could happen is that every single one of you quit your job and every single AIDS agency should fold up shop. That way, there'd be so many dead bodies everywhere that people like lily-livered Bill Clinton and pompous windbag Mario Cuomo would finally be unable to locate their front doors. And then maybe, just maybe, they'd finally be forced into seriously starting the research for a cure."

April 25, 1993.

"I look around and I realize: This is part of a great American tradition."
—Keith Meinhold

"No more homophobia. Let's respect people, protect people. Everyone is someone."
—Reverend Jesse Jackson

"Everything I do and many things I have said make perfectly clear my support of the gay rights movement."
—Madonna

Brent Nicholson Earle and Mel Cheren, October 10, 1992. Cheren is "The Godfather of Disco," credited with inventing the twelve-inch dance single. He also founded Twenty-four Hours for Life, a nonprofit group for AIDS education and fundraising. His partner Earle is an activist and athlete who started AREA (American Run for the End of AIDS) over a decade ago; he has run around the entire country, covering nine thousand miles in twenty months, raising three hundred thousand dollars. They made the shirts that they are wearing, showing the names of their friends who died of AIDS.

Eric von Schmetterling representing ADAPT, April 25, 1993.

Quilt for Sergeant Leonard Matlovich displayed on the mall on October 21, 1989. He also wrote his own gravestone, seen here on April 25, 1993; denied burial at Arlington National Cemetery, he was interred in the Congressional cemetery.

By the time the Stonewall riots took place, homosexuality, as a part of public discourse, was old hat in San Francisco. The first documented gay bar was The Dash, which opened in 1908; a lesbian bar, Mona's, opened in 1936. But, before World War II, most social life took place in private homes. A gay scene emerged during the war, though, as millions of young men heading into the Pacific theater converged there. After the war, many dishonorably discharged homosexual veterans returned to San Francisco. Bars like the Black Cat, in addition to serving drinks and offering a dance space, became centers of information, news, and meetings.

As a direct result of the McCarthy hearings, in 1951 the Los Angeles-based Mattachine Society opened chapters in Oakland, Berkeley, and San Francisco. In 1955, the nation's first organized lesbian group, the Daughters of Bilitis, had its first meeting in San Francisco, led by organizers Phyllis Lyon and Del Martin. The years 1959 to 1961 brought increased police harassment against the gay community. Because of the beat movement and the publicity given to the homophile groups, the establishment decided to move against these two "deviant" groups. Inspired by pressure against homosexuals, drag queen José Sarria made a run for city supervisor in 1961 and gained between 5,600 and 7,000 votes. Scandals involving the payoffs made by gay bars to the city police—commonly known as the Gayola Scandals—also disturbed gay voters.

On New Year's Eve in 1964, a gay and lesbian dance held at California Hall was raided by the police. Although the incident didn't receive the same national attention as the later Stonewall riots, it was no less significant. More than five hundred individuals bought tickets to the event, the first dance sponsored by the Council on Religion and the Homosexual. Guests entered the hall past kleig lights and police photographers. From 9 P.M. on, the police found a reason to enter the hall every few minutes, using as an excuse the need to monitor fire and liquor license laws. Finally, Herb Donaldson and Evander Smith, two lawyers, challenged the constant interruptions. A small fracas broke out and arrests were made. "The police were brutal," said Hal Call, one of the event organizers and a Mattachine official. The next day, several clergymen held a news conference calling on the city to accept homosexuals as human beings. Charges against the gays were later dropped, and the judge in the case lectured the arresting officers for their overzealousness.

During the '70s, San Francisco became a mecca for gays and lesbians seeking a freer, open lifestyle. It was the first city to elect an openly gay person to govern

San Francisco

it, when Harvey Milk, after two losses, was elected supervisor in 1977. He was assassinated by disgruntled city official Dan White a year later. During the 1980s, barriers continued to fall. In 1981, the nation's first gay bank, Atlas Savings and Loan, opened, and Woody Tennant come out as the city's first openly gay cop. The next year, the first Gay Games took place. California Hall activist Herb Donaldson was appointed by Governor Jerry Brown to a Municipal Court seat in 1983. During the 1984 Democratic National Convention, one hundred thousand people participated in a gay-rights march.

San Francisco has evolved to be at the forefront of national gay life, with its vibrant Castro district, publications like the *Advocate* and the *Sentinel*, and many gay city officials. Although there are still many hurdles to overcome, it has become a beacon for a successful integration of a gay community into a straight society.

San Francisco photos and text ©1994 by Rink Foto.

Gay Parade, 1978. Led by drummer Bobby Pace, this group was so incensed by Anita Bryant's public statements against homosexuality that they decided to carry a display featuring her photo along with Hitler, Stalin, the KKK, and Idi Amin.

Castro Street, 1985. The intersection of 18th and Castro Streets is considered the center of San Francisco's gay community.

"I always think of the Castro area as being like old Jerusalem and I see the areas surrounding it as being the new Jerusalem, in the sense that there is a spiritual or religious significance for gay people overlooking this little stretch."

—Tony Marbotta, social scientist

Lesbian Marchers, 1977. This was one of the first appearances of large numbers of lesbians in the Gay Parade; its name was changed to the Lesbian/Gay Parade three years later.

"Many of the lesbians [in San Francisco] came out of the feminist movement, because many of their issues were being addressed there. Women were coming out both because they really were lesbians and for political reasons, as sisterhood.

"In general, West Coast lesbians were politically correct and did not wear makeup. They were devoted to cultural feminism and mother god, recreating the historical matriarchy. In New York, they dressed in a more feminine way."
—Deborah Wolf, author, The Lesbian Community

The Castro Street Fair, 1981. This annual fair was founded by Harvey Milk in 1974; it has since grown to attract over one hundred thousand people.

Spectators at the Castro Street Fair, 1981.

The AIDS/ARC Vigil, 1987. This vigil was held to protest government inaction against the AIDS crisis. At right, writer Mike Hippler interviews Frank Bert, one of the pair of original protesters who chained themselves to City Hall. The flag at left is the "Don't Tread on Me" symbol from the American Revolution.

"I recognize the important contributions the gay and lesbian community has made to improving the quality of life for all San Franciscans."　　　　—*Mayor Frank Jordan*

The AIDS/ARC Vigil, 1987. Prominent lesbian and gay activists chained themselves to San Francisco's Old Federal Building. Front row, l to r: Greg Day, Barbara Cameron, Pat Norman, Ken McPherson.

Harvey Milk's Inauguration, 1977. Mayor George Moscone and Milk greet admirers.

AIDS Awareness Week, 1983. Mayor Diane Feinstein announcing the first AIDS Awareness Week. Posing with her were members of the group People with AIDS (l to r): Mark Feldman, Gary Walsh, Bobbi Campbell, Bobby Reynolds, Roger Lyon. All are since deceased. Feinstein would spend more than $50 million on HIV during her term as mayor.

The Harvey Milk Club at the 1982 Lesbian/Gay Parade. Named for the slain city official, this group was led by gay supervisor Harvey Britt, at left in the back seat. Joining him was Phil Burton, a local congressman, who courted gay and lesbian votes by appearing in the parade.

Dan White Suicide, 1985. Gay activists dance a can-can at the corner of Market and Castro Streets in celebration of Dan White's suicide (since officially designated as Harvey Milk Plaza by the City of San Francisco). L to r: Jack Fertig (Sister Boom Boom), Rick Turner, Arthur Evans (The Red Queen), Ben Gardiner, Steve Cain.

Randy Shilts signs his book, *And the Band Played On*, for Lieutenant Governor Leo McCarthy, 1987.

"Harvey Milk achieved in death what he might not have achieved in life. He saw his death as part of the process. . . . It was part of the political theater of his life. You really can't separate his death from his message." ——*Randy Shilts*

Bathhouse, 1981. An employee of the Ritch Street Baths relaxes at the bath's Minoan Pool, a large, steaming hot tub. This bathhouse was later closed in the wake of the AIDS epidemic.

"There was a gay voting bloc as early as the 1950s on the West Coast. The history of it is that a lot of gay men and women in the Pacific Theater in World War II were dishonorably discharged and went to live in the Bay Area. They had job protection—the many who worked for the city government—but were harassed in bars. They blended into the communities in which they lived and developed gay neighborhoods. They didn't achieve real political clout until later—Harvey Milk being elected was an early high point—but there was a tacit understanding that there was a viable gay and lesbian vote in San Francisco long before Stonewall." —Deborah Wolf, author, The Lesbian Community

Safe Sex Monitor at the Academy, 1984. In accordance with Judge Wonder's legal statement, posted at the Academy, sex monitors were assigned to ensure that unsafe sex did not occur at the club. The monitor carried a three-foot-long flashlight. Warnings were posted and safe sex information was dispensed.

Mobile VD Clinic, 1982. In the late '70s and early '80s, a mobile VD clinic visited Castro Street to provide free disease screening. Since 1984, the rate of VD infection has dropped so much that the van service has been suspended. This drop is attributed to safer sex practices inspired by the fear of AIDS.

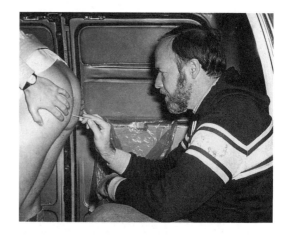

Two participants at the California Motorcycle Club's Annual Carnival, 1982. An intense kiss is shared by this couple who just met at the club's carnival. They introduced themselves, clamped their nipples together with one chain, and then kissed. The event used to have a "back room," but it was discontinued when safe sex practices were introduced in the San Francisco gay community.

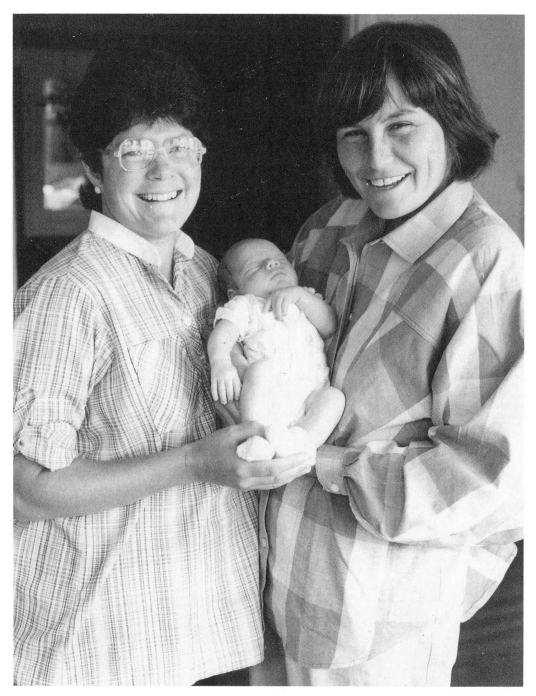

Lesbian parents, 1986. L to r: Judge Mary Morgan, Benji, and City of San Francisco Supervisor Roberta Achtenberg. Achtenberg has since been appointed to HUD by President Clinton, fulfilling a campaign promise to appoint more lesbians and gays to government posts. Mary Morgan is now a Washington, D.C. attorney.

The Sisters of Perpetual Indulgence protest the Pope's visit to San Francisco, 1987. This spiritual group of male and female "nuns" dress up to raise money for charity. They led a weeklong series of events against the Pope's visit, including a huge street protest only a block away from the Mission district church where the Pope appeared. L to r: Sister Blanche (gender female), Sister Vicious Power Hungry Bitch, and Sister Dana Van Iniquity.

"President Clinton said more than once that in his America we don't have a person to waste. By virtue of the kinds of people he has included in this administration, he has observed that truth again and again."
                                                                    —*Roberta Achtenberg*

The Day of Disaster, 1991. Beginning with the chaining of a BART (subway) car to the station platform, this daylong protest of government inaction concerning AIDS ended with a performance by dancing pink-shrouded figures in San Francisco's City Hall. The dancers are Mark Wang and Paul Ortiz.

"The 1992 film 'Edward II' was described by some reviewers as the ultimate defiant homosexual movie. I don't mind it being described as that. . . . I can't think of any more defiant artist [than Christopher Marlowe]. Marlowe's written statements are all revolutionary. His athiesm was a capital offense at the time. His homosexuality was very up front and aggressive. And I think all the problems are still going on and still with us."
                                                                    —Derek Jarman, director

World AIDS Day, 1992. World AIDS Day/Day Without Art commemorated the effect of AIDS on the artistic community. Artist Rudy Lemcke draws chalk lines around another artist at the DeYoung Museum.

Act-Up at the 1989 Lesbian/Gay Parade. Act-Up is one of the most vocal participants in the annual parades. In 1989, Announcer Hank Plante, the parade's MC and an openly gay local television personality, failed to announce Act-Up, showing that at least a portion of the gay/ lesbian community is still uncomfortable with this group's radical stance.

"I've always monitored social progress by the calls I get from the media. It began as media silence regarding AIDS and gay issues and now we're the flavor of the month. People are fascinated by us now. The trick is to turn a trendy preoccupation with gays into a steady civil rights matter." —Jay Blotcher, Queer Nation

SELECT BIBLIOGRAPHY
Edited by Gloria S. McDarrah

Abbott, Sidney, and Barbara Love. *Sappho Was a Right-on Woman: A Liberated View of Lesbianism*. New York: Stein & Day, 1972.

Adam, Barry D. *The Rise of a Gay and Lesbian Movement*. New York: Macmillan, 1987.

Adelman, Marcy, ed. *Long Time Passing: Lives of Older Lesbians*. Boston: Alyson Publications, 1986.

Altman, Dennis. *Homosexual Oppression and Liberation*. Rev. ed. New York: New York University Press, 1993.

——. *The Homosexualization of America, The Americanization of the Homosexual*. New York: St. Martin's Press, 1982.

Baetz, Ruth. *Lesbian Crossroads*. New York: William Morrow, 1980.

Bailey, Derrick Sherwin. *Homosexuality and the Western Christian Tradition*. London: Longmans, Green, 1955.

Balka, Christie, and Andy Rose, eds. *Twice Blessed: On Being Lesbian or Gay and Jewish*. Boston: Beacon Press, 1991.

Barrett, Martha Barron. *Invisible Lives: The Truth about Millions of Women-Loving Women*. New York: William Morrow, 1989.

Bawer, Bruce. *A Place at the Table*. New York: Poseidon, 1993.

Bell, Alan, and Martin Weinberg. *Homosexualities: A Study of Diversities among Men and Women*. New York: Simon & Schuster, 1978.

Bell, Alan, Martin Weinberg, and S. K. Hammersmith. *Sexual Preference: Its Development in Men and Women*. Bloomington: Indiana University Press, 1981.

Benjamin, Harry. *The Transsexual Phenomenon*. New York: Julian Press, 1966.

Berger, Raymond M. *Gay and Gray: The Older Homosexual Man*. Champaign: University of Illinois Press, 1982.

Bergler, Edmund. *Disease or Way of Life?* New York: Hill & Wang, 1956.

Bernstein, Eduard. *On Homosexuality*. Dublin: Athol Books, 1977.

Berube, Allan. *Coming Out under Fire, The History of Gay Men and Women in World War II*. New York: Free Press, 1990.

Berzon, Betty. *Positively Gay: New Approaches to Gay and Lesbian Life*. Rev. ed. Berkeley, CA: Celestial Arts, 1993.

Blumenfeld, Warren J., ed. *Homophobia: How We All Pay the Price*. Boston: Beacon Press, 1992.

Blumenfeld, Warren J., and Diane Raymond. *Looking at Gay and Lesbian Life*. Rev. ed. Boston: Beacon Press, 1989.

Boswell, John. *Christianity, Social Tolerance and Homosexuality*. Chicago: University of Chicago Press, 1981.

Boughner, Terry. *Out of All Time: A Gay and Lesbian History*. Boston: Alyson Publications, 1988.

Bray, Alan. *Homosexuality in Renaissance England*. Boston: Gay Men's Press, 1988.

Brown, Howard. *Familiar Faces, Hidden Lives: The Story of Homosexual Men in America Today*. New York: Harcourt Brace Jovanovich, 1976.

Browning, Frank. *The Culture of Desire: Paradox and Perversity in Gay Lives Today*. New York: Crown, 1993.

Bullough, Vern L. *Homosexuality: A History*. New York: New American Library, 1979.

———. *Sexual Variance in Society and History*. New York: John Wiley & Sons, 1976.

Burch, Beverly. *On Intimate Terms: The Psychology of Difference in Lesbian Relationships*. Champaign: University of Illinois Press, 1993.

Cant, Bob, and Susan Hemmings. *Radical Records: Personal Perspectives on Lesbian and Gay History*. New York: Routledge, 1988.

Castle, Terry. *The Apparitional Lesbian*. New York: Columbia University Press, 1993.

Churchill, Wainwright. *Homosexual Behavior among Males: A Cross-cultural and Cross-species Investigation*. Englewood Cliffs, NJ: Prentice-Hall, 1967.

Clark, Don. *Living Gay*. Berkeley, CA: Celestial Arts, 1979.

Clunis, D. Merilee, and G. Dorsey Green. *Lesbian Couples*. Seattle: Seal Press, 1988.

Comstock, Gary D. *Violence against Lesbians and Gay Men*. New York: Columbia University Press, 1991.

Corea, Gena. *The Invisible Epidemic: The Story of Women and AIDS*. New York: HarperCollins, 1992.

Cory, Donald Webster. *The Homosexual in America: A Subjective Approach*. New York: Greenburg, 1951.

Cory, Donald Webster, and John P. LeRoy. *The Homosexual and His Society*. New York: Citadel Press, 1963.

Costello, John. *Virtue Under Fire: How World War II Changed Our Social and Sexual Attitudes*. Boston: Little, Brown, 1985.

Cox, Cece, Lisa Means, and Lisa Pope. *One Million Strong, The 1993 March on Washington for Lesbian, Gay, and Bi Equal Rights*. Boston: Alyson Publications, 1993.

Cruikshank, Margaret. *The Gay and Lesbian Liberation Movement*. New York: Routledge, 1992.

Curb, Rosemary, and Nancy Manahan, eds. *Lesbian Nuns: Breaking Silence*. New York: Warner Books, 1986.

Curry, Hayden, and Dennis Clifford. *A Legal Guide for Lesbian and Gay Couples*. 4th ed. Berkeley, CA: Nolo Press, 1986.

D'Emilio, John. *Sexual Politics, Sexual Communities: The Making of a Homosexual Minority in the United States, 1940-1970*. Chicago: University of Chicago Press, 1983.

Deming, Barbara. *Remembering Who We Are*. Tallahassee, FL: Naiad Press, 1989.

Diamant, L. *Homosexual Issues in the Workplace*. Bristol, PA: Hemisphere Publishing, 1993.

Dickens, Homer. *What a Drag: Men as Women and Women as Men in the Movies*. New York: Quill, 1984.

Dover, Kenneth J. *Greek Homosexuality*. Cambridge: Harvard University Press, 1978.

Duberman, Martin B. *About Time: Exploring the Gay Past*. Rev. ed. New York: NAL-Dutton, 1991.

———. *Cures: A Gay Man's Odyssey*. New York: Penguin, 1991.

———. *Stonewall*. New York: Dutton, 1993.

Duberman, Martin, Martha Vicinus, and George Chauncey, eds. *Hidden from History: Reclaiming the Gay and Lesbian Past*. New York: New American Library, 1989.

Dworkin, Andrea. *Letters from a War Zone*. Brooklyn, NY: Lawrence Hill Books, 1992.

Dyer, Kate, ed. *Gays in Uniform: The Pentagon's Secret Reports*. Boston: Alyson Publications, 1990.

Dynes, Wayne R. *Encyclopedia of Homosexuality*. New York: Garland Publishing, 1990.

Dynes, Wayne R., and Stephen Donaldson, eds. *Studies in Homosexuality*. 13 vols. New York: Garland Publishing, 1992.

Ebert, Alan. *The Homosexuals*. New York: Macmillan, 1977.

Eidsmoe, Joan. *Gays and Guns: The Case against Homosexuals in the Military*. Lafayette, LA: Huntington House, 1993.

Ellenzweig, Allen. *The Homoerotic Photograph: Male Images from Durieu/Delacroix to Mapplethorpe*. New York: Columbia University Press, 1992.

Ellis, Havelock. *Sexual Inversion*. Vol. 2, *Studies in the Psychology of Sex*. Philadelphia: F. A. Davis, 1915.

Faderman, Lillian. *Odd Girls and Twilight Lovers: A History of Lesbian Life in Twentieth-Century America*. New York: Columbia University Press/Penguin, 1993.

———. *Surpassing the Love of Men: Romantic Friendship and Love between Women from the Renaissance to the Present*. New York: William Morrow, 1981.

Faderman, Lillian, and B. Eriksson, eds. and trans. *Lesbian-Feminism in Turn-of-the-Century Germany*. Tallahassee, FL: Naiad Press, 1980.

Fass, Diana. *Inside-Out: Lesbian Theories, Gay Theories*. New York: Routledge, 1991.

Foucault, Michel. *The History of Sexuality*. New York: Vintage Books, 1978.

Fumento, Michael. *The Myth of Heterosexual AIDS*. New York: Basic Books, 1990.

Gallo, Robert, M.D. *Virus Hunting: AIDS, Cancer, and the Human Retrovirus*. New York: Basic Books, 1991.

Garber, Marjorie. *Vested Interests: Cross-Dressing and Cultural Anxiety*. New York: Routledge, 1991.

Gooding, Caroline. *Trouble With the Law? A Legal Handbook for Lesbians and Gay Men*. London: Gay Men's Press, 1993.

Greenberg, David F. *The Construction of Homosexuality*. Chicago: University of Chicago Press, 1988.

Gross, Larry. *Contested Closet: The Politics and Ethics of Outing*. Minneapolis: University of Minnesota Press, 1993.

Harry, Joseph, and William B. Devall. *The Social Organization of Gay Males*. New York: Praeger, 1979.

Heger, Heinz. *The Men with the Pink Triangle*. Boston: Alyson Publications, 1980.

Herdt, Gilbert. *Gay Culture in America: Essays from the Field*. Boston: Beacon Press, 1993.

Herdt, Gilbert, and Andrew Boxer. *Children of the Horizons: How Gay and Lesbian Teens Are Leading a New Way Out of the Closet*. Boston: Beacon Press, 1992.

Hite, Shere. *The Hite Report on Male Sexuality*. New York: Alfred A. Knopf, 1981.

Hocquenghem, Guy. *Homosexual Desire*. Trans. Daniella Dangoor. Rev. ed. Durham, NC: Duke University Press, 1993.

Hoffman, M. *The Gay World: Male Homosexuality and the Social Creation of Evil*. New York: Bantam, 1969.

Humphreys, Laud. *Out of the Closets: The Sociology of Homosexual Liberation*. Englewood Cliffs, NJ: Prentice-Hall, 1972.

Jarman, Derek. *At Your Own Risk*. New York: Overlook Press, 1993.

———. *Dancing Ledge*. New York: Overlook Press, 1993.

———. *Modern Nature*. New York: Overlook Press, 1994.

Jay, Karla, and Allen Young, eds. *Out of the Closets: Voices of Gay Liberation*. New York: Douglas, 1972.

Johnston, Jill. *Lesbian Nation*. New York: Simon & Schuster, 1973.

———. *Mother Bound*. New York: Alfred A. Knopf, 1983.

———. *Paper Daughter*. New York: Alfred A. Knopf, 1985.

Karlen, A. *Sexuality and Homosexuality*. New York: Norton, 1971.

Katz, Jonathan. *Gay American History: Lesbians and Gay Men in the U.S.A.* New York: Crowell, 1976.

———. *Gay-Lesbian Almanac: A New Documentary*. New York: Harper & Row, 1983.

Kennedy, Elizabeth L., and Madeline D. Davis. *Boots of Leather, Slippers of Gold: The History of a Lesbian Community*. New York: Routledge, 1993.

King, Edward. *Gay Men Fighting AIDS*. Fort Lauderdale, FL: Cassell Communications, 1993.

Kinsey, Alfred C., Wardell B. Pomeroy, and Clyde E. Martin. *Sexual Behavior in the Human Female*. Philadelphia: W. B. Saunders, 1953.

———. *Sexual Behavior in the Human Male*. Philadelphia: W. B. Saunders, 1948.

Kirk, Marshall, and Hunter Madsen. *After the Ball: How America Will Conquer Its Fear and Hatred of Gays in the 90s*. New York: Doubleday, 1989.

Kitzinger, Celia, and Rachel Perkins. *Changing Our Minds: Lesbian Feminism and Psychology*. New York: New York University Press, 1994.

Klein, Fritz, and Timothy J. Wolf. *Two Lives to Lead: Bisexuality in Men and Women*. New York: Harrington Park Press, 1985.

Lauritzen, John, and David Thorstad. *The Early Homosexual Rights Movement, 1864-1935*. New York: Times Change Press, 1974.

Leinen, Stephen. *Gay Cops*. New Brunswick, NJ: Rutgers University Press, 1993.

Leonard, Arthur S. *Sexuality and the Law: An Encyclopedia of Major Legal Cases*. New York: Garland Publishing, 1993.

LeVay, Simon. *The Sexual Brain*. Cambridge: MIT Press, 1993.

Levine, M.P. *Gay Men: The Sociology of Male Homosexuality*. New York: Harper & Row, 1979.

Lewis, Sasha G. *Sunday's Women: A Report on Lesbian Life Today*. Boston: Beacon Press, 1979.

Licata, Salvatore J., and Robert P. Peterson, eds. *Historical Perspectives on Homosexuality*. Binghamton, NY: Haworth Press, 1981.

Lobel, Kerry. *Naming the Violence: Speaking Out about Lesbian Battering*. Seattle: Seal Press, 1986.

Marcus, Eric. *Is It a Choice? Answers to 300 of the Most Frequently Asked Questions about Gays and Lesbians*. San Francisco: Harper, 1993.

———. *The Struggle for Gay and Lesbian Equal Rights, 1945-1990: An Oral History*. New York: HarperCollins, 1992.

Marmor, J., ed. *Homosexual Behavior: A Modern Reappraisal*. New York: Basic Books, 1980.

Marotta, Toby. *The Politics of Homosexuality*. Boston: Houghton Mifflin, 1981.

Martin, Dell, and Phyllis Lyon. *Lesbian/Woman*. Rev. ed. New York: Bantam Books, 1983.

May, Rollo. *Sex and Fantasy: Patterns of Male and Female Development*. New York: W. W. Norton, 1980.

McCubbin, Bob. *The Gay Question: A Marxist Appraisal*. Northridge, CA: Worldview Publishers, 1993.

McNaught, Brian. *Gay Issues in the Workplace*. New York: St. Martin's Press, 1993.

McWhirter, David P., and Andrew M. Mattison. *The Male Couple: How Relationships Develop*. Englewood Cliffs, NJ: Prentice-Hall, 1984.

Miller, Neil. *In Search of Gay America: Women and Men in a Time of Change*. New York: HarperCollins, 1990.

———. *Out in the World: Gay and Lesbian Life from Buenos Aires to Bangkok*. New York: Vintage Books, 1993.

Mohr, Richard D. *Between Men–Between Women: Lesbian and Gay Cultures*. New York: Columbia University Press, 1988.

——. *Gay Ideas: Outing and Other Controversies*. Boston: Beacon Press, 1993.

Money, John. *Gay, Straight, and In-Between: The Sexology of Erotic Orientation*. New York: Oxford University Press, 1988.

Morris, Jan. *Conundrum: An Extraordinary Narrative of Transsexualism*. New York: Henry Holt, 1986.

Murphy, Lawrence R. *Perverts by Official Order: The Campaign Against Homosexuals by the United States Navy*. New York: Harrington Park Press, 1988.

Myron, N., and C. Bunch, eds. *Lesbianism and the Women's Movement*. Baltimore, MD: Diana Press, 1975.

Nelson, Emmanuel S., ed. *Contemporary Gay American Novelists: A Bio-bibliographical Critical Sourcebook*. Westport, CT: Greenwood Press, 1993.

Newton, Esther. *Cherry Grove, Fire Island: 60 Years in America's First Gay and Lesbian Town*. Boston: Beacon Press, 1993.

Paglia, Camille. *Sexual Personae*. New Haven: Yale University Press, 1993.

Plant, Richard. *The Pink Triangle: The Nazi War against Homosexuals*. New York: Henry Holt, 1986.

Plummer, Ken, ed. *Modern Homosexualities: Fragments of Lesbian and Gay Experience*. New York: Routledge, 1993.

Puterbaugh, Geoff, ed. *Twins and Homosexuality: A Casebook*. New York: Garland, 1991.

Reinisch, June Machover. *The Kinsey Institute New Report on Sex: What You Must Know to Be Sexually Literate*. New York: St. Martin's Press, 1990.

Reyes, Karen Westerbred, comp., and Lorena Fletcher Farrell, ed. *Lambda Gray: A Practical, Emotional and Spiritual Guide for Gays and Lesbians Who Are Growing Older*. Van Nuys, CA: Newcastle Publishing, 1992.

Rodgers, Bruce. *Gay Talk: A Dictionary of Gay Slang*. New York: Paragon Books, 1979.

Roof, Judith. *A Lure of Knowledge: Lesbian Sexuality and Theory*. New York: Columbia University Press, 1993.

Rowse, Alfred L. *Homosexuals in History: A Study of Ambivalence in Society, Literature and the Arts*. New York: Carroll & Graf, 1983.

Rubenstein, William B. *Lesbians, Gay Men, and the Law*. New York: New Press, 1993.

Ruitenbeck, Hendrick M. *Psychoanalysis and Female Sexuality*. Raleigh: North Carolina University Press, 1966.

——. *Psychoanalysis and Male Sexuality*. Raleigh: North Carolina University Press, 1966.

——., ed. *The Problem of Homosexuality in Modern Society*. New York: Dutton, 1963.

Russell, Ina, ed. *Jeb and Dash: A Diary of Gay Life, 1918-1945*. New York: Faber & Faber, 1993.

Russo, Vito. *The Celluloid Closet: Homosexuality in the Movies*. New York: Harper & Row, 1987.

Rutledge, Leigh W. *The Gay Book of Lists*. Boston: Alyson Publications, 1987.

——. *The Gay Decades: From Stonewall to the Present–the People and Events that Shaped Gay Lives*. New York: Penguin, 1992.

———. *Unnatural Quotations*. Boston: Alyson Publications, 1988.

Sedgwick, Eve Kosofsky. *Tendencies*. Durham, NC: Duke University Press, 1993.

Sherman, Suzanne. *Lesbian and Gay Marriage: Private Commitments, Public Ceremonies*. Philadelphia: Temple University Press, 1992.

Shilts, Randy. *And the Band Played On: Politics, People, and the AIDS Epidemic*. New York: St. Martin's Press, 1987.

———. *Conduct Unbecoming, Gays and Lesbians in the U.S. Military*. New York: St. Martin's Press, 1993.

———. *The Mayor of Castro Street: The Life and Times of Harvey Milk*. New York: St. Martin's Press, 1982.

Signorile, Michelangelo. *Queer in America*. New York: Random House, 1993.

Silverstein, Charles. *Man to Man: Couples in America*. New York: William Morrow, 1981.

Smith-Rosenberg, Carroll. *Disorderly Conduct: Visions of Gender in Victorian America*. New York: Oxford University Press, 1985.

Steakley, James D. *The Homosexual Emancipation Movement in Germany*. New York: Arno, 1975.

Steffan, Joseph. *Honor Bound: A Gay American Fights for the Right to Serve His Country*. New York: Random House, 1992.

Stein, Arlene, ed. *Sisters, Sexperts, Queers: Beyond the Lesbian Nation*. New York: NAL-Dutton, 1993.

Stern, Phyllis N. *Lesbian Health: What Are the Issues?* Bristol, PA: Hemisphere Publishing, 1993.

Stryker, Jeff, ed., and Albert R. Jonsen. *The Social Impact of AIDS*. Washington, DC: National Academy Press, 1993.

Teal, Donn. *The Gay Militants*. New York: Stein and Day, 1971.

Tielman, Rob, Aart Hendriks, and Evert van der Veen. *Bisexuality and HIV-AIDS: A Global Perspective*. Buffalo, NY: Prometheus Books, 1993.

———. *The Third Pink Book: A Global View of Lesbian and Gay Liberation and Oppression*. Buffalo, NY: Prometheus Books, 1993.

Timmons, Stuart. *Trouble with Harry Hay: Founder of the Modern Gay Movement*. Boston: Alyson Publications, 1991.

Tripp, C. A. *The Homosexual Matrix*. New York: McGraw-Hill, 1975.

Van Gelder, Lindsay. *Are You Two . . . Together?* New York: Random House, 1991.

Warner, Michael, ed. *Fear of a Queer Planet: Queer Politics and Social Theory*. Minneapolis: University of Minnesota Press, 1993.

Warren, C. A. B. *Identity and Community in the Gay World*. New York: John Wiley & Sons, 1974.

Webber, Winni S. *Lesbians in the Military Speak Out*. Northboro, MA: Madwoman Press, 1993.

Weinberg, George. *Society and the Healthy Homosexual*. New York: St. Martin's Press, 1972.

Weinberg, Martin S., and Colin J. Williams. *Homosexuals and the Military: A Study of the Less Than Honorable Discharge*. New York: Harper & Row, 1971.

———. *Male Homosexuals, Their Problems and Adaptations*. New York: Oxford University Press, 1974.

Weiss, Andrea, and Greta Schiller. *Before Stonewall: The Making of a Gay and Lesbian Community*. Tallahassee, FL: Naiad Press, 1988.

Wolf, Deborah Goleman. *The Lesbian Community*. Berkeley and Los Angeles: University of California Press, 1979.

Wolff, C. *Love between Women*. New York: Harper & Row, 1972.

Wolinsky, Marc, and Kenneth Sherrill. *Gays and the Military*. Princeton, NJ: Princeton University Press, 1993.

Young, Allen. *Gays under the Cuban Revolution*. San Francisco: Grey Fox, 1982.

Index

Page numbers of photographs are in italics